Since late 1943 the German army had adopted a completely defensive strategy where the frontline was held by infantry formations equipped with large numbers of automatic weapons. If this line was threatened, or actually broke, an armoured reserve would cut off the enemy spearhead and plug the gap. In practice the armoured units were often scrapped together from disparate formations and this was a form of warfare at which the Germans were masters. A key component of this strategy was the heavy tank battalion of schwere Panzer-Abteilung. In the first book in this series *Tiger I and II Tanks: German Army and Waffen-SS Eastern Front 1944* we examined the development of these powerful tanks and the technical modifications that were incorporated into production until the end of 1944. We also looked at the table of organisation for a heavy tank battalion introduced in June 1944 which was not superseded until the following November. As all units of the German army were built, equipped or refitted following detailed tables and charts known as Kriegsstärkenachweisungen, usually abbreviated to KstN, and examples of these are shown in this book, including the November instructions, on pages 9, 12, 16 and 54.

The tenth book in the TankCraft series *Tiger I: German Army Heavy tank Southern Front North Africa, Sicily and Italy 1942-1945* dealt with the earlier model tanks and the relevant modifications and also the various KstN beginning with the August 1942 table.

This book focuses on the Tiger tanks that attempted to hold back the British and American armies during the last few months and weeks of the war in battles that seemed to increase in their intensity as the end drew closer. As mentioned elsewhere in this book, relatively few Tigers fought on the Western Front during the period covered by this book. Of the Tiger I and Tiger II tanks which had taken part in the battles of late 1944, all were either in repair or with units that were being rebuilt in January 1945. In March, when the Americans and British were both conducting major offensive operations, Oberbefehlshaber West could call on just thirty operational Tigers. It must have been an unlucky Allied tank crew that came upon one of these monsters yet such was its reputation that every German tank was thought to be a Tiger and every gun an 88.

The scarcity of these tanks is one reason, I suspect, for the paucity of photographs and the reader will notice that the great majority of the images in this book are of captures or disabled tanks. Somewhat ironically this was in fact a great help when preparing the illustrations as many of the abandoned Tigers were photographed from several angles.

Said to have been photographed near Schierke in the Harz region during the spring of 1945 this Tiger II is almost certainly one of the tanks of schwere Panzer-Abteilung 507. Although of indifferent quality this image is interesting in that it shows the single-link track and 18-tooth drive sprocket. These modifications were introduced in March 1945 and could have only been fitted to a very few tanks as just thirty Tigers were accepted by the Heereswaffenamt in that month. The front mudguards are, however, the earlier pattern, without the reinforcing rib, which were supposed to have been superseded in the same month.

Photographed near Petit Spa on the Amblève River in early January 1945 this Tiger II of 3.Kompanie, schwere SS-Panzer-Abteilung 501 was the last tank lost by the battalion during the fighting in the Ardennes when it was abandoned here on Christmas day 1944.

Although various locations have been given for this image I believe that this may be one of two Tigers of the schwere Panzer-Abteilung 506 lost on 13 January 1945 in a fight with tanks of the US 6th Armoured Division near the Moinet farm, and not the town of Moinet, just off the road from Villers-la-Bonne-Eau to Lutramange. Note the lack of Zimmerit paste and the factory-applied camouflage suggesting that this is one of the fifteen tanks received by the battalion between 12 September and 13 December 1944. What may have been an earlier set of numbers appears to have been painted over on the turret side.

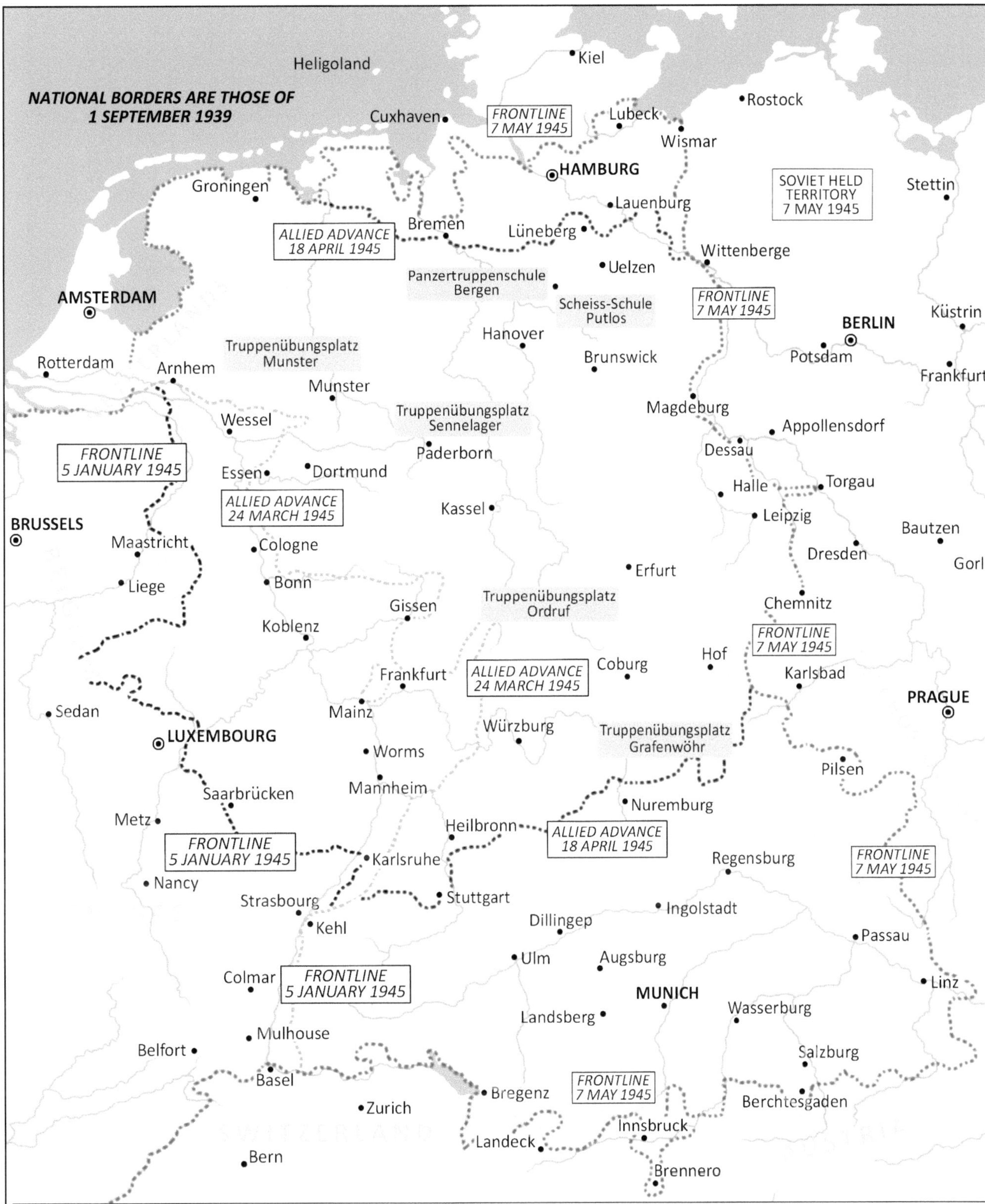

Our map depicts the situation on the Western Front from the beginning of 1945 until the end of the war. Note that the front as shown for 7 may 1945 is in fact the line of demarcation as agreed with the Soviets and some US Army units had penetrated beyond this, particularly in southern Germany and Czechoslovakia, only to be ordered to withdraw. The failure of the Wacht am Rhein offensive in the Ardennes, which began on 16 December 1944, an the subsequent Operation Nordwind, launched on the last day of the year, saw the loss of much of the armoured reserve that could have been used in the defence of the west. The timeline below outlines the significant events of the first months of 1945.

1 January 1945. *The Tigers of schwere Panzer-Abteilung 506 support an attack on Michamps near Bastogne.*

3 January 1945. *Schwere SS-Panzer-Abteilung 501, with thirty operational tanks, makes repeated attacks against the Bastogne corridor. Although ultimately successful, the Germans do not have the resources to exploit their advance and Allied counterattacks begin on the northern side of the Ardennes salient.*

5 January 1945. *With Operation Nordwind bogged down, a supplementary operation codenamed Sonnenwende begins and units of Oberkommando Öberrhein manage to create a bridgehead on the Rhine between Strasbourg and Hagenau.*

8 January 1945. *As the German units in the Ardennes begin to withdraw, two Tigers of schwere SS-Panzer-Abteilung 501 are left with 340.Volksgrenadier-Division to act as a rearguard.*

9 January 1945. *In what is virtually the last gasp of Operation Nordwind, Kampfgruppe Feuchtinger launches an attack against Hatten, south of Oldenburg.*

12 January 1945. *Operation Nordwind is brought to a halt less than 20 kilometres from Strasbourg. British and US Army forces link up near La-Roche-en-Ardenne, north-west of Houffalize.*

17 January 1945. *US Army tanks breakthrough east of Bastogne slamming into schwere Panzer-Abteilung 301. Three Tigers are abandoned by their crews.*

22 January 1945. *Units of Heeresgruppe G and Oberkommando Öberrhein link up but are unable to force a crossing of the Moder River.*

28 January 1945. *The Germans withdraw from the Ardennes salient.*

4 February 1945. *The last German troops leave Belgium.*

7 February 1945. *The Germans destroy the floodgates in the Ruhr valley in the area west of Cologne, preventing the use of assault bridges.*

8 February 1945. *British and Canadian troops launch an offensive into the Reichswald.*

9 February 1945. *The last Rhine bridge is destroyed in the Colmar Pocket after much of 19.Armee has been evacuated. Hauptmann Heiligenstadt, the commander of schwere Panzer-Abteilung 506, is taken prisoner.*

10 February 1945. *US units capture the last of the Ruhr dams.*

12 February 1945. *British and Canadian troops capture Cleve.*

17 February 1945. *US 3rd Army breaks through the Siegfried Line and advances into Germany.*

23 February 1945. *US 9th Army attacks from the Roer bridgehead towards the Hürtgen Forest but is bogged down in savage fighting.*

28 February 1945. *US units in the Hürtgen Forest break through near Erkelenz, west of Cologne, at great cost.*

6 March 1945. *Cologne surrenders.*

7 March 1945. *The Rhine bridge at Remagen is captured intact.*

10 March 1945. *Generalfeldmarschall Kesselring replaces von Rundstedt as Oberbefehlshaber West.*

12 March 1945. *Kampfgruppe Dunker attempts to defend Beckum, south-east of Münster, with four Tigers rendered immobile due to lack of fuel. These tanks had been intended for schwere Panzer-Abteilung 506 but were appropriated by elements of 116.Panzer-Division*

14 March 1945. *US Army units cross the Moselle.*

15 March 1945. *Attempts by the Americans to expand the Remagen bridgehead fail. Two days later the bridge collapses.*

20 March 1945. *Saarbrücken falls to the Allies.*

22 March 1945. *Units of the US 3rd Army cross the Rhine at Oppenheim south of Mainz against ineffective German resistance.*

23 March 1945. *Elements of Panzergruppe Hudel, including the Tigers of schwere Panzer-Abteilung 506, attack the Remagen bridgehead. British and Canadian units begin their assault across the Rhine above the Ruhr.*

24 March 1945. *Panzergruppe Hudel's counterattack near Eitorf east of Bonn fails.*

25 March 1945. *British troops capture Wesel after an aerial bombardment almost completely destroys the town. On the following day Main and Darmstadt fall to US troops*

Photographed at some time after the end of the war, perhaps as late as 1947, this Tiger II of schwere Panzer-Abteilung 507 is also shown on page XX shortly after it was abandoned in Osterode on 24 April 1945. The company number of 402 can be seen clearly seen here as can the seemingly dark outline of the turret Balkenkreuz. This tank is also depicted in the Camouflage and Markings section.

Although this photograph was taken in Hungary at the conclusion of the Lake Balaton battles it gives a good impression of the appearance of the Tigers of schwere SS-Panzer-Abteilung 501 in early 1945. A Tiger II with this number, 334, is known to have been lost of 22 December 1944 near La Gleize during the fighting in the Ardennes and this tank is almost certainly one of the vehicles taken over from the battalion's 1.Kompanie or one of the six replacements received on 26 January1945. This tank is also shown and discussed on page 17 of the Camouflage and Markings section of this book.

27 March 1945. *As the Allies approach, the managing directors of Henschel and Wegmann are informed that all industrial works in the Kassel arae are to be thoroughly destroyed. Several crews of schwere Panzer-Abteilung 508, which had recently returned from Italy, are formed into a Kampfgruppe with a single Tiger and six Panthers. After fierce fighting US Army units capture Aschaffenburg.*

28 March 1945. *British troops begin their drive towards the Elbe as the US Army captures Marburg and Limburg.*

31 March 1945. *The last thirteen Tigers to be assembled leave the Henschel plant. Two Tiger I and three Tiger II tanks of Panzer-Lehr- und Ausbildungs-Abteilung 'Tiger' at Paderborn are taken over by crews from 3.Kompanie, schwere Panzer-Abteilung 424 and schwere Panzer-Abteilung 508 respectively. At least one of the Tiger II tanks was an early production vehicle with the Porsche turret.*

1 April 1945. *Panzergruppe Paderborn, an ad-hoc unit scraped together from the staff of Panzer-Schule Paderborn, attacks US units at Nordborchen, north of the Dortmund to Kassel road. A single Tiger is able to hold up a US Army task force west of Borchen before withdrawing. Two US Armies link up at Lippstadt cutting off over 300,000 German troops in the Ruhr area.*

2 April 1945. *The British 7th Armoured Division reaches the Dortmund-Ems canal and over the next week the Allies capture Recklinghausen, Fulda and Karlsruhe on the upper Rhine. The commander of Panzergruppe Paderborn, Hauptmann Uckert, is taken prisoner.*

4 April 1945. *After an almost token resistance the last German troops in Kassel surrender. The survivors of Kampfgruppe Dettmar, with one Tiger, reach the German lines at Veldrom.*

9 April 1945. *Kampfgruppe Schulze, with just eleven tanks including six Tigers, attacks the US positions near Wietersheim losing more than half its strength.*

11 April 1945. *The commander of schwere Panzer-Abteilung 507 reports that his battalion has just one operational Tiger. Tanks and infantry of Kampfgruppe Grosan, including sailors from the 2.Marine-Infanterie-Division supported by two Tiger I tanks, attack British positions at Engehausen near Buchholz where they manage to hold the enemy advance for two days. Weimar, Essen, Bochum and Goslar are captured by the Americans. The British take Celle, near Hannover, cutting the road to Hamburg. US Army units reach Schweinfurt.*

12 April 1945. *Hauptmann Scharfe, the new commander of Panzergruppe Paderborn, reports that all his tanks have either been destroyed or are inoperable. Hauptmann Römer, commanding schwere Panzer-Abteilung 506, reports that just one of his tanks has enough fuel to move under its own power.*

13 April 1945. *The last Tiger of Kampfgruppe Schulze, after running out of fuel, is destroyed by its crew. The remaining tanks, in their last action, attack a US command post at Baringhausen, west of Hannover. Elements of Panzer-Division Clausewitz, the last German armoured division formed during the war, launch a surprise attack against British units in the area of Ülzen-Verssen, inflicting heavy casualties. The US 3rd Army captures Erfurt.*

14 April 1945. *The last tanks of Kampgruppe Grosan attack British units at Ahlften on the Halburger Strasse north of Soltau. Withdrawing through Bassel, one Tiger runs out of fuel and is left behind as a static defence position. On the same day, the British reach Bremen and US units capture Gera and Bayreuth.*

15 April 1945. *Arnhem is captured by the Canadians.*

17 April 1945. *British units attempt to outflank Soltau but are repulsed by the lone Tiger of Kamfgruppe Grosan left in Bassel. The last Tigers of 3.Kompanie, schwere Panzer-Abteilung 510 are abandoned between Braunlage and Elend, south-east of Goslar.*

18 April 1945. *The tanks of Panzer-Division Clausewitz drive the British from their positions around Wittingen. The US Army takes Magdeburg, Düsseldorf and Nürnberg. American units advance into western Czechoslovakia. The British capture Ülzen and Lüneburg.*

19 April 1945. *Near Thale, in the Harz Mountains, Oberleutnant Leonhardt orders 3.Kompanie, schwere Panzer-Abteilung 511 to disband after destroying the company's last vehicles. British troops launch an attack on Bremen. Leipzig and Halle fall to the Americans.*

21 April 1945. *Elements of Panzer-Division Clausewitz capture the Gifhorn-Brome road south of Wittingen, surprising US units who mistake them for Americans. French units capture Stuttgart although the Germans continue to resist around Elbingerode in the Harz Mountains.*

22 April 1945. *US 7th Army captures a bridge across the Danube. British troops reach Bremen. The next day, Dessau and Harburg are cleared of German troops and Frankfurt is captured.*

24 April 1945. *British and Canadian troops enter Bremen. US units cross the Danube at Dillingen and capture Ulm.*

25 April 1945. *US and Soviet units meet on the Elbe at Torgau south-west of Berlin.*

26 April 1945. *US troops take Regensburg on the Danube.*

28 April 1945. *The Canadians capture Emden and Wilhelmshaven, while US units take Augsburg and reach the Austrian border.*

29 April 1945. *A single Tiger of Panzer-Division Clausewitz halts the advance of the 3rd Royal Tank Regiment. British troops cross the Elbe near Hamburg. The US 7th Army reaches Munich.*

30 April 1945. *Hitler commits suicide appointing Grossadmiral Karl Dönitz as his successor. US and Soviet units meet at Ellenburg, south of Berlin.*

1 May 1945. *The single Tiger attached to Panzer-Division Clausewitz, which had stopped the British armoured advance near Wittingen on 29 April, again manages to halt a complete tank regiment outside Schwarzenbek, east of Hamburg.*

2 May 1945. *The British reach Lübeck on the Baltic coast.*

3 May 1945. *Generalmajor Alwin Wolz, the garrison commander, declares Hamburg an open city and surrenders to the British. US troops reach the Brenner Pass on the Italian border.*

4 May 1945. *Admiral Hans-Georg von Friedeburg, representing the German government, arrives at Field Marshal Montgomery's headquarters to surrender all German forces in Holland, North-west Germany and Denmark. The US 7th Army takes Innsbruck, Salzburg and Berchtesgarten.*

5 May 1945. *The US 3rd Army takes Pilsen in Czechoslovakia and prepares to drive towards Prague.*

7 May 1945. *Generaloberst Jodl as OKW Chief of Staff, signs Germany's unconditional surrender. All operations are to cease at one minute after midnight on the following day.*

The ruins of the massive Henschel und Sohn plant at Kassel photographed in May 1945. The very late production Tiger II turret in the centre ground is also shown on the inside back cover.

Despite its perceived faults, few would argue against the proposition that the impression made on Allied tank crews and infantrymen by the Tiger tanks was out of all proportion to the number actually engaged in the fighting. For the month of March 1945 Oberbefehlshaber West reported that just thirty Tiger I and Tiger II tanks in total were available for operations and while this figure rose to thirty-four for April, including one immobile Tiger II pressed into service, these figures are dwarfed by number of tanks the British and American forces could call upon. In fact, by the spring of 1945 much of the burden of the defence in the west was increasingly carried by depleted tank and infantry divisions, fighting as ad-hoc Kampfgruppen, often supported by the old men of the Volkssturm and the boys of the Hitler Youth. Nevertheless, Allied intelligence reports and unit diaries consistently mistake humbler German tanks for the fearsome Tiger as do, less forgivably, a number of modern publications. The following are short operational histories of the Tiger units engaged in combat in the west during the last months of the war. The earlier histories of some of the battalions listed here are covered in the first title in this series *Tiger I and Tiger II Tanks: German Army and Waffen-SS Eastern Front 1944.*

Schwere Panzer-Abteilung 501. Formed in May 1942, the battalion's first and second companies served in North Africa, surrendering to Allied forces almost exactly one year later (1).

The battalion was reformed in September 1943 and served on the Eastern Front, losing all its tanks by 5 July 1944 in the devastating Russian summer offensive. The battalion was once again reformed, this time with Tiger II tanks, and returned to the east in early August 1944 and spent the next months fighting around Baranow Sandomierski in southern Poland.

On 21 December 1944 the battalion was renamed schwere Panzer-Abteilung 424 to differentiate it from the premier Waffen-SS Tiger battalion that had been renumbered from 101 to 501 (see below). By January 1945, schwere Panzer-Abteilung 424 had been reduced to a handful of Tigers supplemented by a number of Panthers, Pzkw IV tanks and Jagdpanzer IV tank destroyers scrapped together from various maintenance depots and in the following month the battalion was disbanded. The remnants of the first and second companies were used to form schwere Panzerjäger-Abteilung 512, equipped with Jagdtiger tank destroyers, and in March and April the crews of 3.Kompanie, which had been retraining at Paderborn in Germany under the command of Oberleutnant Busch, were incorporated into a Kampfgruppe made up from the tanks of Panzer-Ersatz-und Ausbildungs-Abteilung 500.

Busch's command contained two Tiger I tanks, one Panther and one Pzkw IV tank and fought against the rapidly advancing British. One of the Tigers was destroyed in the fighting at Paderborn railway station but much of the Kampfgruppe was able to reach Höxter, between Paderborn and Northeim, were they surrendered to the Allies.

Schwere Panzer-Abteilung 502. Formed in May 1942 the battalion served on the Eastern Front and was renamed schwere Panzer-Abteilung 511 in January 1945. Earlier, in November 1944, after months of almost continuous combat in the east, the battalion's third company, commanded by Hauptmann Christoph Leonhardt, handed over their six remaining tanks to Schwere Panzer-Abteilung 510 and returned to Sennelager in Germany.

On the last day of March 1945 the company received eight Tiger II tanks from the Henschel factory at Kassel and saw some action in the surrounding area. Official American sources state that advance elements of US 3rd Army were severely mauled by seven Tiger II tanks between Fritzlar and Kassel on the same day although the Germans were forced back by heavy artillery fire. On 2 April, to the south of Kassel, the Americans were able to knock out one Tiger and damage another which had been supporting an attack made by Panzergrenadier-Ersatz-und-Ausbildungs-Bataillon 15. Separated from their infantry, the tanks continued towards the south but ran into a devastating artillery barrage that destroyed a further two Tigers with direct hits.

A second German assault in the same area was also beaten back by heavy artillery fire. It should be noted, however, that the fighting here was extremely confused and the German records are incomplete or non-existent and the Tigers of schwere Panzer-Abteilung 510 were also active in this area.

A number of tanks were able to reach the Harz Mountains, over 100 kilometres to the east, but on 19 April 1945, near Thale, south-west of Magdeburg, Hauptmann Leonhardt disbanded the company.

Schwere Panzer-Abteilung 506. Formed in May 1943 the battalion served in the east until August 1944 when the crews were transferred to the Ohrdruf training grounds in Germany to re-equip with Tiger II tanks.

The battalion fought in the Netherlands, most notably around Arnhem, and in early December 1944 the Tiger I tanks of Panzer-Kompanie Hummel were attached as the battalion's fourth company. From 21 December 1944, under Major Eberhard Lange, the battalion was committed to the Ardennes Offensive, attached to 6.Panzerarmee together with schwere Panzer-Abteilung 301 (Funklenk).

The battalion took part in the fighting around Lentzweiler on the Elsborn Ridge and supported the attack of Grenadier-Regiment 294 along the Schönberg road.

Notes

1. 3.Kompanie was renamed as the tenth company of Panzer-Regiment Grossdeutschland in July 1943.

Photographed near Bardenberg, north of Aachen, in late 1944 this Tiger II of schwere Panzer-Abteilung 506 is one of at least two tanks of the battalion disabled here by US Army units. Note the remains of the Zimmerit coating on the hull glacis confirming that this tank was built before September 1944.

On the last day of 1944, the battalion was involved on an unsuccessful assault on the town of Bastogne. During the first week of January 1945 the Tigers supported an attack made by elements of 12.SS-Panzer-Division, destroying fifteen US Army Sherman tanks in a single action near Wardin but the main objective, the town of Longchamps north of Bastogne, remained in American hands. By the middle of the month German units in the Ardennes were on the defensive and schwere Panzer-Abteilung 506, with seventeen operational tanks, was committed to delaying actions between Houffalize and the German frontier. Also at this time Major Lange was replaced by Hauptmann Heiligenstadt on the orders of the the 5.Panzerarmee commander, Generaloberst von Manteuffel, who blamed Lange for the battalion's lack of success (1).

In early February 1945 the battalion was withdrawn to the area between Niedersdorf and Wallersheim, which was at that time just a few short miles from the front, to rest and refit.

On 9 February, in what must have been a severe blow, the new commander together with Hauptmann Wacker, who had led 2.Kompanie at Arnhem, and Leutnant Bopp were all captured while on a limited reconnaissance mission. Nevertheless, on the same day the battalion's tanks supported separate attacks by 2.Panzer-Division and 340.Volksgrenadier-Division to the north and west of Prüm. On 16 February 1945 the battalion's fourth company, with five serviceable Tiger I tanks, was permanently detached and returned to its previous status and as an independent company.

On 15 March 1945 the battalion reported that just fifteen tanks were on hand, with only two of those being considered operational, but seven Tigers were handed over from schwere SS-Panzer-Abteilung 501 five days later and on 22 March a company of Jagdtiger tank destroyersfrom schwere Panzerjäger-Abteilung 512 was attached to the battalion (2). An allocation of thirteen new Tiger II tanks never reached the battalion and although the fate of most of these vehicles is uncertain, at least four took part in the defence of Beckum with Kampfgruppe Dunker as immobile pill-boxes due to a complete lack of fuel.

From late March 1945 the battalion, with the remainder of schwere Panzerjäger-Abteilung 512 and the Jagdpanthers of Panzerjäger-Abteilung 654, formed part of Panzergruppe Hudel, fighting in the Remagen Bridgehead. Commanded by Major Helmut Hudel, who had served with Panzer-Regiment 7 and schwere Panzer-Abteilung 508, this was the most powerful German armoured force in the area but was still unable to prevent the Americans from expanding their bridgehead across the Rhine.

During the first week of April 1945 schwere Panzer-Abteilung 506, with twelve operational tanks, was attached to Panzer-Brigade 106 and fought around Brunskapple and Elpe, south of the Dortmund to Kassel road, in an effort to deny the towns to the US 9th Infantry Division and subsequently fell back towards Werdohle, where a single Tiger was tasked with holding the battalion's front.

By 13 April 1945, with most tanks out of fuel, the survivors had reached the forest near Iserlohn, south of Münster, and on the following day Hauptmann Jobst-Christoph von Römer, who had assumed command when Hauptmann Heiligenstadt was captured, formally disbanded the battalion.

Notes

1. Lange's defence, that he had been ordered to commit his tanks in a piecemeal fashion, was not without foundation. An experienced officer, he had led the battalion on the Eastern Front from November 1943 and during the fighting in the west.

2. The Jagdtiger company only remained with the battalion until 26 March 1945.

SCHWERE PANZER-ABTEILUNG 506, LATE 1944-EARLY 1945

On 8 December 1944 the Tiger I tanks of schwere Panzer-Kompanie Hummel were attached to this formation and served as the battalion's fourth company until February 1945. The assumption of KstN 1176e, the organisation superceded by the 1 June 1944 order, for 4.Kompanie is purely speculative on my part but possible given that schwere Panzer-Kompanie Hummel was originally an Alarmheit, or emergency, company raised from training units. The Erkunderzug had been a scouting unit dropped in 1943 and its personnel absorbed by the Aufklärungszug and the Pionierzug (reconaissance and engineer platoons).

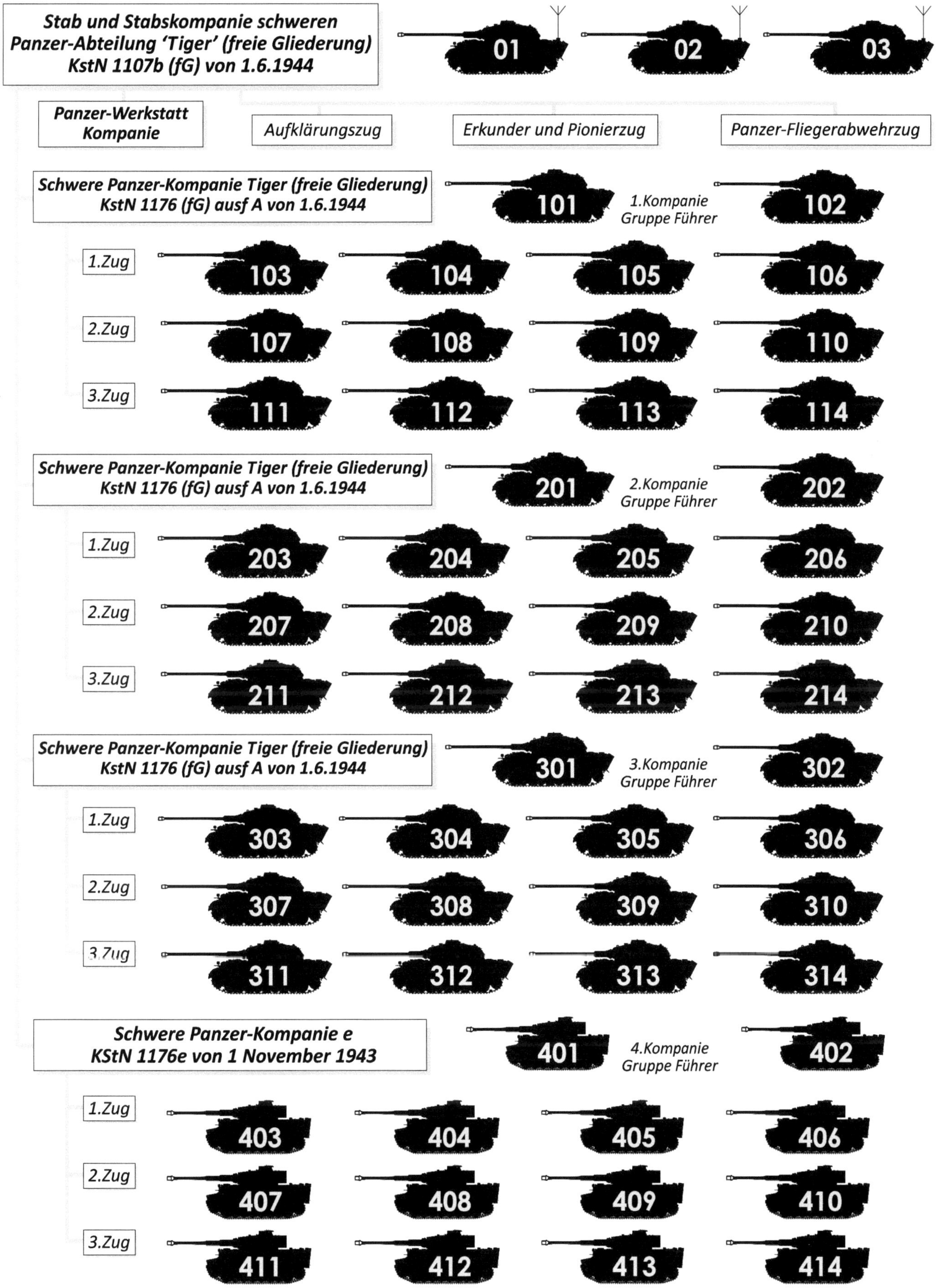

Above: Photographed near Gereonsweiler, about 5 kilometres east of Geilenkircken, this Tiger II of 2. Kompanie, schwere Panzer-Abteilung 506 was captured intact shortly before the start of the Ardennes Offensive. In other photographs of this tank the company number 211 is clearly visible on the turret side. This vehicle is also shown and discussed on apge 24 of the Camouflage and Markings section. At right: A later production Tiger II, evidenced by the rain guard over the sight aperture which was introduced in November 1944, of Panzer-Abteilung 506 photographed near Marmecke, south-east of Schmallenberg. This tank was disabled here on 11 April 1945 while supporting an assault made by 338.Infanterie-Division.

Photographed near Harste, north-west of Göttingen, this Tiger II was probably disabled here in late March or early April 1945. Of note are the single-link tracks and 18-tooth drive sprocket introduced into production in March. This tank, and its unusual camouflage scheme, is also discussed on page 22.

Schwere Panzer-Abteilung 507. Originally formed in May 1943 the battalion went through a number of reorganisations before it was eventually sent to the Eastern Front in March 1944.

The battalion remained in the east until mid-February 1945 when the second and third companies were transferred to Truppenübungsplatz Sennelager in Germany to be re-equipped with the Tiger II, while 1.Kompanie remained at the front for some weeks with just two operational tanks.

By the end of March 1945 the battalion had received twenty-one Tiger II tanks and three Jagdpanther tank destroyers. The latter were allocated to 2.Kompanie, commanded by Oberleutnant Dr. Maximilian Wirsching together with six of the Tigers while the remaining twelve Tigers were concentrated in 3.Kompanie under Hauptmann Wolf Koltermann, an experienced and highly decorated veteran. It is not known what vehicles, if any, the headquarters possessed although some light cars and halftracks had survived the fighting in the east and accompanied the battalion to Sennelager in mid-February 1945. The battalion commander, Major Fritz Schröck, accompanied the tanks of 3.Kompanie during the fighting near Castle Hamborn while 2.Kompanie was some 8 kilometres away between Dörenhagen and Eggeringhausen and in the short, confused battles which followed it is likely that Major Schröck and his staff remained with this group.

All elements of the battalion were far short of their authorised establishments and 1.Kompanie, which had arrived in Germany during the first week of March, was never to receive any tanks. However, the situation in the west had become so Desperate that the understrength companies in training were thrown into the fighting against units of the advancing US Army. On 30 March 1945 parts of 2.Kompanie supported SS-Regiment Holzer, part of SS-Brigade Westfalen, in an attack west of Dörenhagen and late in the day took up defensive positions in a wooded area near Dahl. After refuelling the tanks moved on to Bad Driburg, about 10 kilometres east of Paderborn. Early on the following day 2.Kompanie, with four Tigers and three Jagdpanthers, attacked enemy positions between Altenbeken and Hamborn, losing three of the Tigers in an ambush.

In the following days the battalion attempted to halt the advance of the US 3rd Armored Division and by 2 April 1945, most of the battalion's tanks had been dispersed and attached to several Kampfgruppen. On 7 April one of the second company's Jagdpanthers and a single Tiger engaged a US armoured unit near Polle and, firing across the Weser River, and managed to destroy seventeen American tanks. Later that day a Jagdpanther was lost and this may have been the last of the original three as no further mention is made of these vehicles in any account I have been able to examine. Indeed, the two Tigers which took part in the defence of the Leine bridge near Göttingen on 9 April 1945 are recorded as the battalion's last surviving armoured vehicles. By 17 April what remained of the battalion had been moved to Prague to be rebuilt and rearmed with Jagdpanzer 38 Hetzer tank destroyers (1).

Notes

1. It seems that only 3.Kompanie received their allocation. The battalion was renamed Panzer-Abteilung 507.

Fighting their way towards the west the survivors surrendered to US Army units at Rosenthal, modern day Rozmital in the Czech Republic, on 12 May 1945 but were all handed back to the Soviets.

SCHWERE HEERES PANZER-ABTEILUNG 507, APRIL 1945

On 30 January 1945 the battalion's second and third companies began moving from the Eastern Front to Sennelager in Germany and by 20 February they had been joined by 1.Kompanie. On 25 February 1945 orders were issued to refit the battalion using the November 1944 organisations shown here and from 9 March a total of twenty-one Tiger II tanks were received, the final six arriving on the last day of the month. In addition, 2.Kompanie was allocated three Jagdpanther tank destroyers which were used to form the third platoon. Although there is no known official record of these vehicles being issued by the Heereszeugamt to this battalion during March or April 1945, the post-war account of former Feldwebel Friedrich Schreiber, who commanded the third platoon, confirms their existence and describes the actions in which they took part in some detail, particularly the fighting around the town of Hofgeismar, about 40 kilometres south-east of Paderborn.

Stab und Stabskompanie
Panzer-Abteilung (freie Gliederung)
KStN 1107(fG) von 1 November 1944

It is not known what vehicles, if any, the headquarters possessed although some light cars and halftracks had survived the fighting in the east and accompanied the battalion to Sennelager in mid-February 1945. This is discussed further in the main text.

Panzer-Werkstatt-Kompanie
KStN 1187b von 1 November 1944

Versorgungs-Kompanie
KStN 1151b(fG) von 1 November 1944

Panzer-Kompanie (freie Gliederung)
KStN 1176(fG) von 1 November 1944

Commanded by Oberleutnant Rudi Beilfuss, 1.Kompanie never received any tanks and remained in Sennelager until 16 April 1945 when the remains of the battalion were transferred to Prague.

Panzer-Kompanie (freie Gliederung)
KStN 1176(fG) von 1 November 1944

The refitting of 2.Kompanie was incomplete when the available tanks were thrown into battle. The company Gruppe Fuhrer, Oberleutnant Maximilian Wirsching commanded one of the Tigers, possibly of the first platoon.

1.Zug
2.Zug
3.Zug

Panzer-Kompanie (freie Gliederung)
KStN 1176(fG) von 1 November 1944

3.Kompanie lacked its two authorised Befehlspanzerwagen for the headquarters, however, the company commander, Hauptmann Wolfgang Koltermann, did lead the his men from one of the available Tigers.

1.Zug
2.Zug
3.Zug

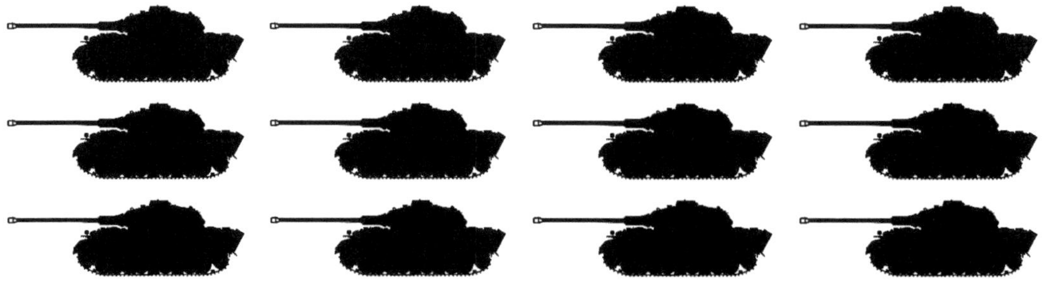

Photographed on 24 April 1945 on the Königsplatz in the town of Osterode am Harz, north-east of Kassel, this Tiger II of schwere Panzer-Abteilung 507 may have been the battalion's last surviving tank. After the war it was towed to an open area on the norther edge of the town to be broken up and is shown there in the photograph on page 4 and in the Camouflage and Markings section on page 22.

Two further views of the late production Tiger II shown of the previous page. These photographs were both taken in Dörgerstrasse before the tank was towed the short distance to the Königplatz. Although the rather unusual company number of 402 is clearly absent in these photographs, there are far to many technical similarities, including the pattern of camouflage, for the identification to be mistaken. Of note are the late-style mudguards in introduced in March 1945.

Schwere Panzer-Abteilung 508. Formed in August 1943 the battalion served on the Italian Front until 12 February 1945 when the remaining fifteen Tigers were handed over to schwere Panzer-Abteilung 504 and the surviving crews returned to Germany.

On 27 March the battalion received a single Tiger and six Panthers and formed a small Kampfgruppe with the surplus crews fighting as infantry. I can find no further mention of these tanks and by April the remnants of the battalion had made their way to Villach in southern Austria by an extremely circuitous route where they began training as artillerymen. The last elements of the battalion surrendered to US Army units on 8 May 1945.

Schwere Panzer-Abteilung 510. Formed on 6 June 1944 from elements of the Kompanieführerschule Versailles and Panzer-Ersatz-Abteilung 500, the battalion served on the Eastern Front, fighting through the Baltic States and Kurland.

In mid-January 1945, 3.Kompanie, under Oberleutnant Hermann Wilhelm Helpup, was transferred to Germany to train on the Tiger II and on 30 March was able to acquire six new tanks directly from the Henschel factory at Kassel. The Tigers were in combat within days in the area around Kassel, taking part in the defence of Fritzlar and Werkel and eventually withdrawing towards Putlos. During the first week of April the Tigers were involved in a number of skirmishes along the Fulda River where one of the tanks was disabled by a hand-held anti-tank weapon and although this vehicle was recovered the Tiger II of Oberfeldwebel Weller broke down near Dahlenrode, between Kassel and Göttingen, and had to be destroyed. This left the company with just four effective tanks.

By 17 April 1945 Hauptmann Helpup ordered his men to abandon the remaining tanks and officially disbanded the company (1).

On the following day in a curious turn of events, Oberfeldwebel Weller and his crew were press ganged into service with SS-Brigade Westfalen and given a Tiger II which had originally belonged to schwere Panzer-Abteilung 507. The tank was eventually disabled after a short battle with a number of US Army tanks and although the crew escaped, Weller was seriously wounded, losing his nose to a shell fragment as he attempted to repair a broken track.

The survivors of 3.Kompanie, schwere Panzer-Abteilung surrendered to British forces on 8 May 1945.

Schwere Panzer-Abteilung 511. See schwere Panzer-Abteilung 502.

Notes

1. I have been unable to confirm the date of Helpup's promotion but it may have been shortly after the company took over the Tigers from Kassel.

Photographed outside Holzhausen, south-west of Kassel, in April 1945 this late production Tiger II is one of the tanks obtained directly from the Henschel plant by 3.Kompanie, schwere Panzer-Abteilung 511. Note the Pilze scoket directly behind the cupola and the two brackets for poison gas detection panels on either side of the lifting eye at the rear of the turret. This vehicle is also shown and discussed on page 24 of the Camouflage and Markings section.

Most sources date this image to either October or November 1944, however, the small sign post which reads Maucke, just below the Geilenkirchen sign, may indicate Kampfgruppe Maucke. This ad-hoc formation was created from elements of 15.Panzergrenadier-Division for the Ardennes Offensive suggesting the correct date is much later. The identification with schwere Panzer-Kompanie Hummel, by both Schneider and Restayn, is probably correct.

Schwere Panzer-Kompanie Hummel. Commanded by Hauptmann Hans Hummel this unit was formed around fourteen Tiger I tanks of Panzer-Ersatz und Ausbildungs-Abteilung 500, a training unit stationed at Paderborn. The company famously fought at Arnhem and on 18 December 1944 was attached to schwere Panzer-Abteilung 506 as the battalion's fourth company.

The company took part in the Ardennes Offensive and reverted to its independent status on 16 February 1945. Although Hauptmann Hummel had been killed in the fighting near Linden in November 1944, official documents from 1945 show that the company retained his name. In late February 1945 tanks from the company supported Panzer-Regiment 33 fighting along the west bank of the Rhine and during the first week of April, with eleven serviceable tanks, the company was attached to Panzer-Brigade 106 in the Ruhr area.

Schwere Panzer-Kompanie Hummel ended the war fighting in the area east of Cologne along the Lenne River between Grevenbrück and Altena.

Panzer-Abteilung (Funklenk) 301. Originally formed in September 1942 the battalion was reorganised between August and October 1944 and allocated thirty-one Tiger I tanks. A number of these vehicles had been rebuilt from damaged tanks and ten were handed over from schwere SS-Panzer-Abteilung 103.

The reformed battalion went into action for the first time on 19 November 1944 near Merzenhausen where the tanks of the first company, which were supported by the Sturmgeschütz III assault guns of Panzer-Kompanie (Funklenk) 319, managed to destroy a number of enemy tanks. During the first week of January 1945 the battalion, with twenty-seven serviceable Tigers, fought against British armoured units in the area between Diergaarde and Braunsrath in the Heinsberg bridgehead near the Dutch border. On 20 January the battalion took part in the unsuccessful counterattack at Bocket, further to the west, losing two Tigers to British anti-tank guns.

On 1 February 1945 the battalion reported that only twelve of the available twenty-three Tigers were operational but within days these were also rendered immobile by a total lack of fuel. Later in February the Tigers took part in the attacks on Erkelenz, on the Heinsberg to Dusseldorf road, and by the end of the month could only field five operational tanks. Further fighting took place in this area and near Sinnersdorf, today an outer suburb of Cologne, two Tigers were destroyed leaving the battalion with four serviceable tanks. In the first week of April 1945 the battalion, with its last three Tigers, was ordered to use the remaining Sprengstoffträger demolition vehicles to destroy the bridge over the Ruhr at Bommern, south-west of Dortmund, but the order was rescinded at the last moment.

On 16 April 1945 the survivors of the battalion withdrew to Sprockhövel, north-east of Wuppertal where the last three serviceable tanks were destroyed by their crews.

.........continued on page 49

SCHWERE PANZER-ABTEILUNG (TIGER-FUNKLENK) 301, LATE 1944

This formation never received its full allocation of tanks, as can be seen from the diagram below, and it seems that one tank was left at Truppenübungsplatz Grafenwöhr in early November when the battalion moved to the front. In early June 1944 new Kreigsstärkenachweisungen, or KstN, were issued for use by Tiger battalions that were at that time being formed, or for existing formations when authorised. Separate KStN, with the suffix ausf B, were introduced for the companies of Tiger-Funklenk units and each was authorised thirty-six Borgward BIV Sprengstoffträger, or demolition carriers, and fourteen tanks. Note that each platoon here only has half the authorised allocation of carriers, more in line with KstN 1176f of 1 February 1944 which the June orders were intended to replace. On 23 October 1944 the battalion received seven Sdkfz 251 halftracks which transported the demolition charges for the BIV ausf C carriers. The Abteilung headquarters was organised as for a Tiger battalion with the addition of a reserve company which held twelve carriers.

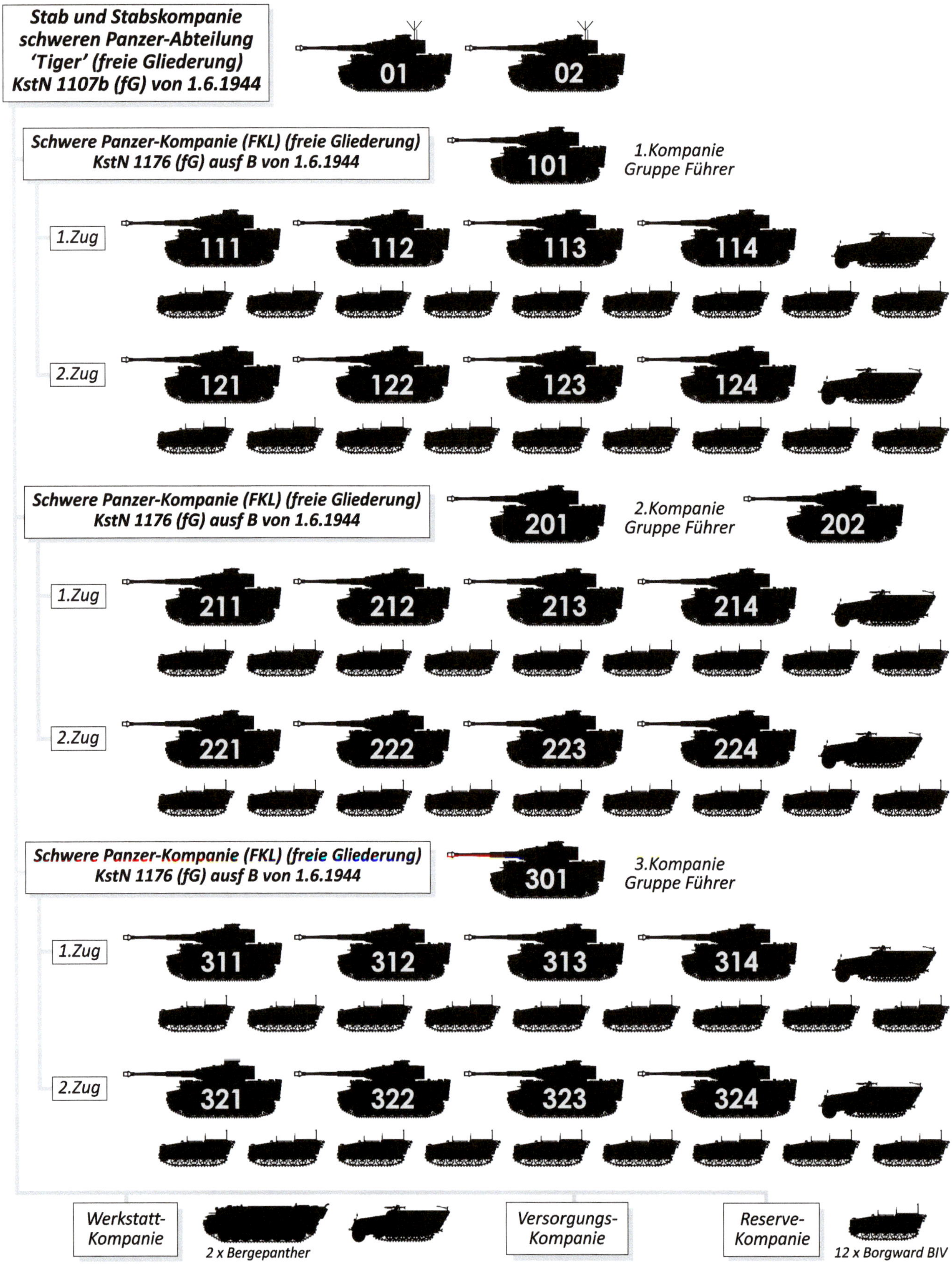

1

3

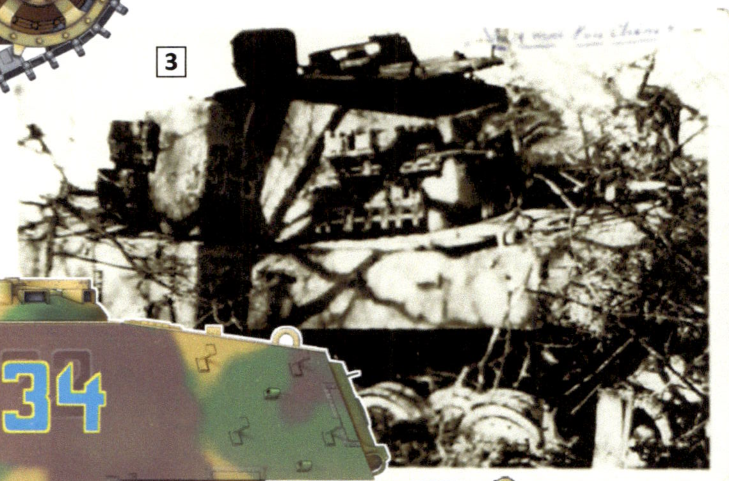

1. **PzKpfw Tiger ausf B. 2.Kompanie, schwere SS-Panzer-Abteilung 501. Early 1945.** Both vehicles on this page were actually photographed in Hungary after the battles around Lake Balaton but as the battalion received only six replacement vehicles between the end of the Ardennes Offensive and the first week of February 1945, when these two companies left Germany for the east, it is reasonably safe to assume that the appearance of the Tigers would not have changed significantly, if at all. The colours used to depict the company numbers are those adopted just prior to the Normandy Campaign and used until the end of the war.

2

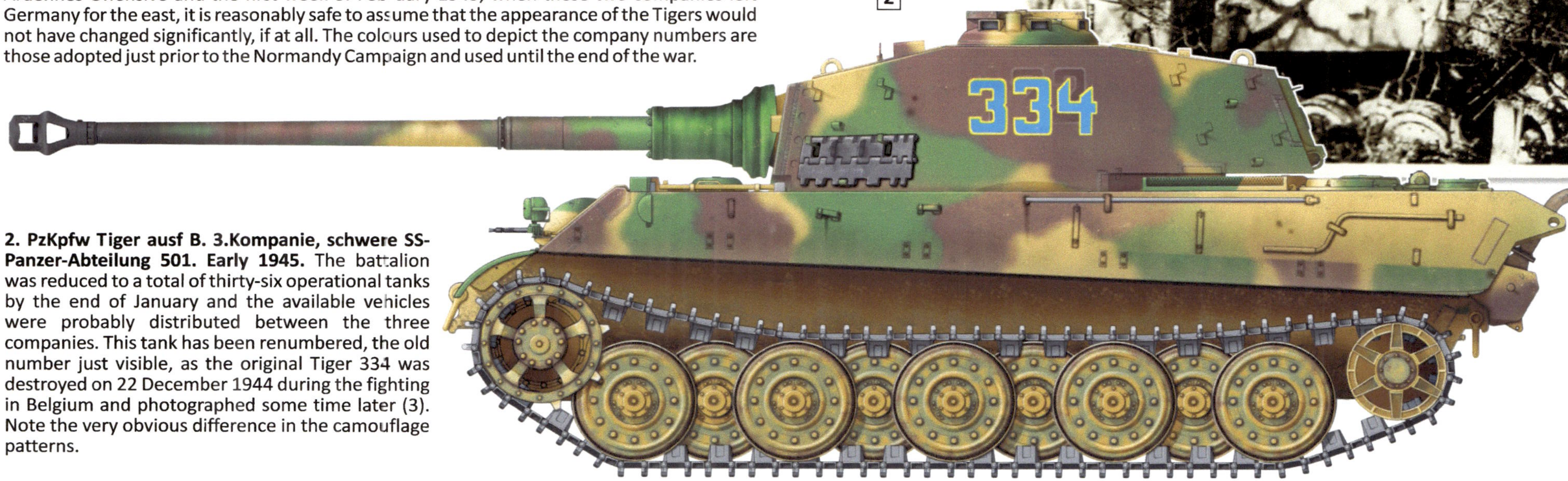

2. **PzKpfw Tiger ausf B. 3.Kompanie, schwere SS-Panzer-Abteilung 501. Early 1945.** The battalion was reduced to a total of thirty-six operational tanks by the end of January and the available vehicles were probably distributed between the three companies. This tank has been renumbered, the old number just visible, as the original Tiger 334 was destroyed on 22 December 1944 during the fighting in Belgium and photographed some time later (3). Note the very obvious difference in the camouflage patterns.

1. Pzkpfw VI ausf E Tiger I. 3.Kompanie, schwere Panzer-Abteilung 301 (Funklenk). Early 1945. This illustration is somewhat conjectural and based on several images of this battalion's tanks as the vehicle in our photograph was almost completely covered in foliage camouflage. The rack fitted to the rear stowage bin (2) was commonly seen of Tigers of this unit although its exact design could vary. The large debris guard over the gun mantlet (3) was another common feature but may have been restricted to the tanks of 2.Kompanie.

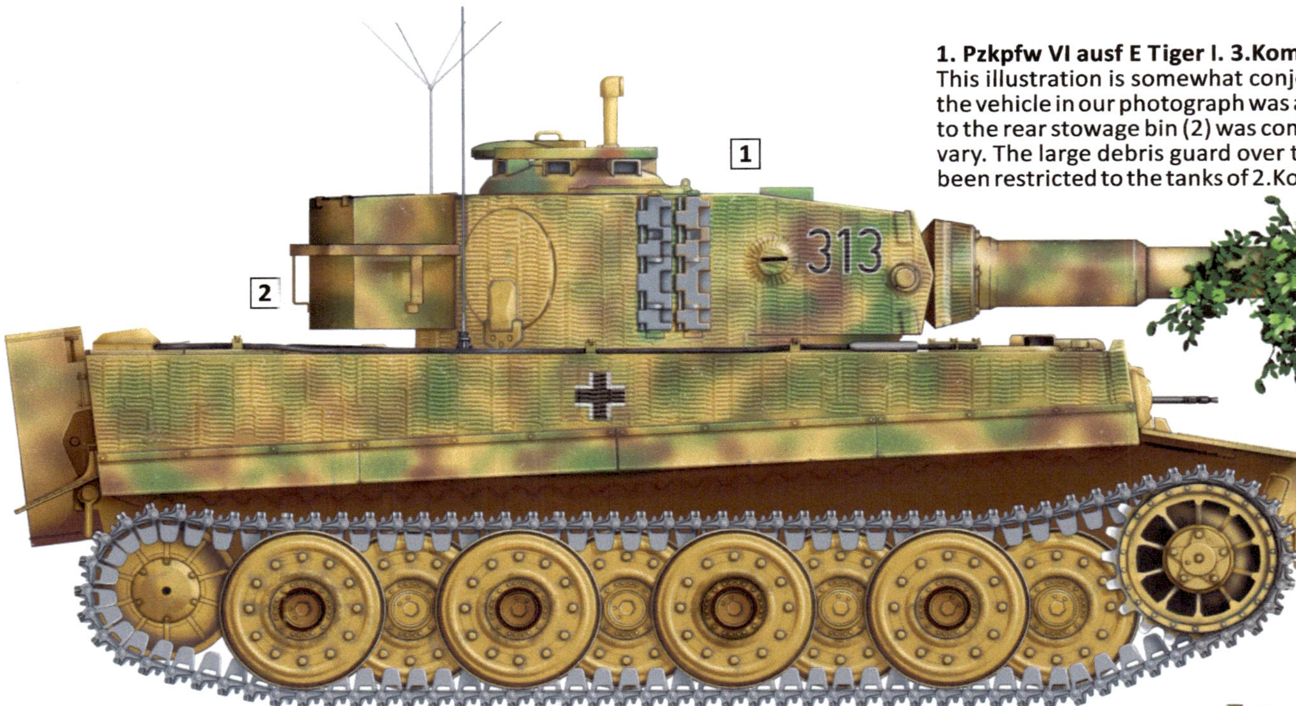

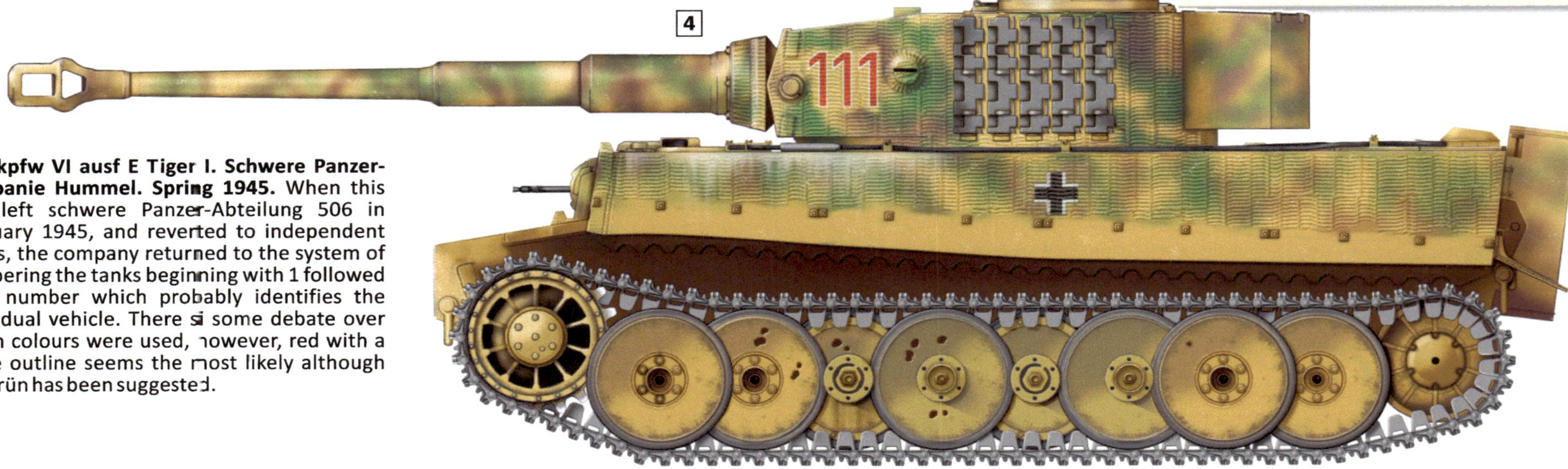

4. Pzkpfw VI ausf E Tiger I. Schwere Panzer-Kompanie Hummel. Spring 1945. When this unit left schwere Panzer-Abteilung 506 in February 1945, and reverted to independent status, the company returned to the system of numbering the tanks beginning with 1 followed by a number which probably identifies the individual vehicle. There si some debate over which colours were used, however, red with a white outline seems the most likely although Olivgrün has been suggested.

1. Pzkpfw VI ausf E Tiger I. Unidentified unit. Early 1945. Photographed in Cologne, shortly after the city was taken by the Allies in March 1945, this tank is typical of the hybrid Tiger I assemblies encountered at this time. The early turret has the so-called drum cupola and the large pistol port on the side towards the rear. Note the remains of the Nebelwurfgeräte bracket just in front of the vision slit. The hull has the steel road wheels introduced from February 1944. Although it has been suggested that this tank may have been operated by schwere Panzer-Abteilung 301 (Fkl), most of these hybrid vehicles seem to have served with ad-hoc units raised from training establishments.

1

3

2

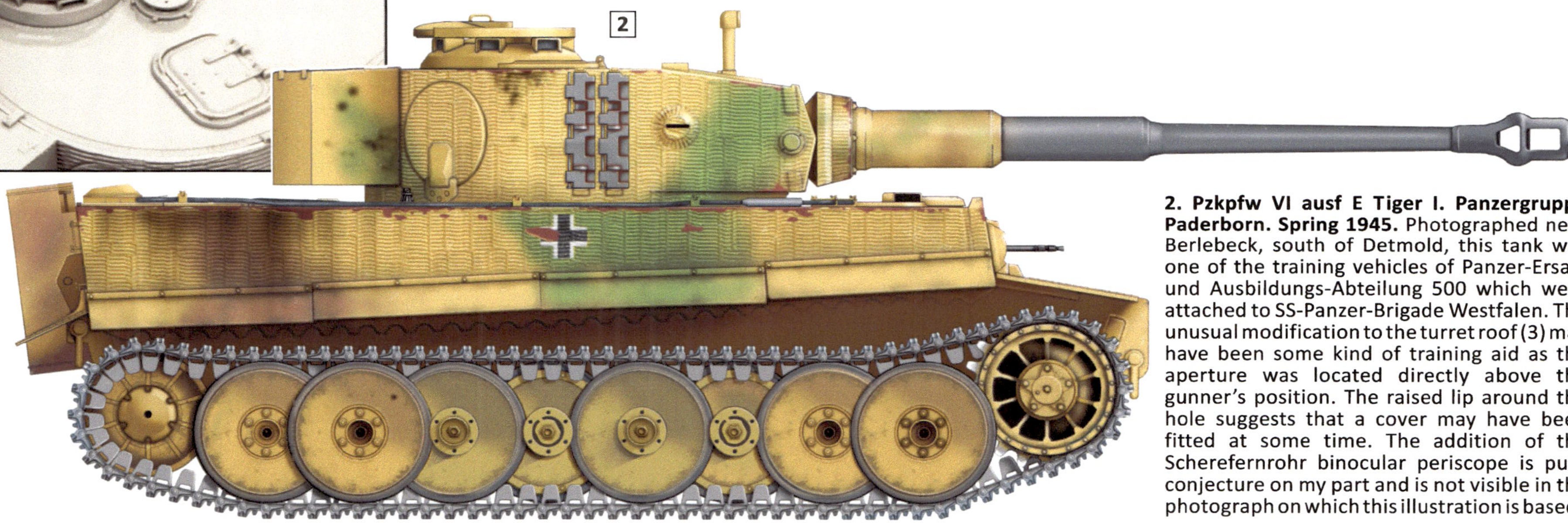

2. Pzkpfw VI ausf E Tiger I. Panzergruppe Paderborn. Spring 1945. Photographed near Berlebeck, south of Detmold, this tank was one of the training vehicles of Panzer-Ersatz und Ausbildungs-Abteilung 500 which were attached to SS-Panzer-Brigade Westfalen. The unusual modification to the turret roof (3) may have been some kind of training aid as the aperture was located directly above the gunner's position. The raised lip around the hole suggests that a cover may have been fitted at some time. The addition of the Scherefernrohr binocular periscope is pure conjecture on my part and is not visible in the photograph on which this illustration is based.

1. Pzkpfw VI ausf E Tiger I. Tigergruppe Fehrmann. Spring 1945. This ad-hoc unit, consisting of six Tiger I tanks, was formed from elements of Panzerschule 1 located at Bergen. All the tanks were numbered in a similar fashion to the example shown here although there is some debate about the colours used. Oberst Wolfgang Schneider, who researched these units extensively, is adamant that the letter F stood for the unit's commander Oberleutnant Rudolf Fehrmann. This formation, and the system of markings, are discussed further in the main text.

1

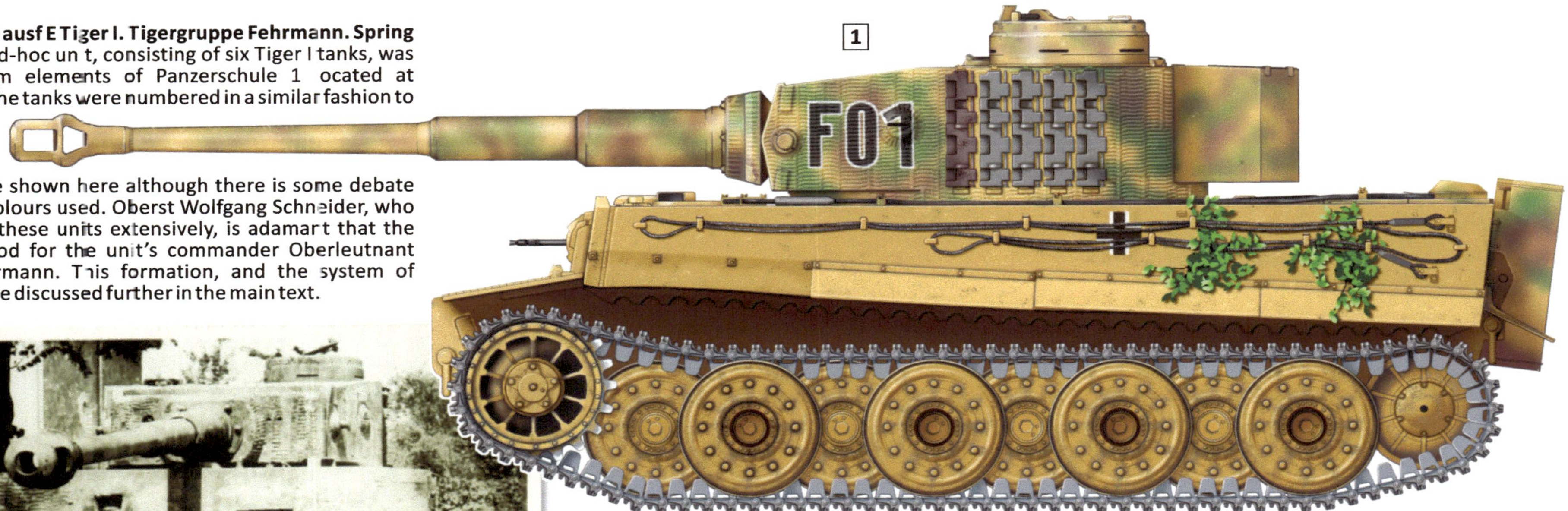

3

2

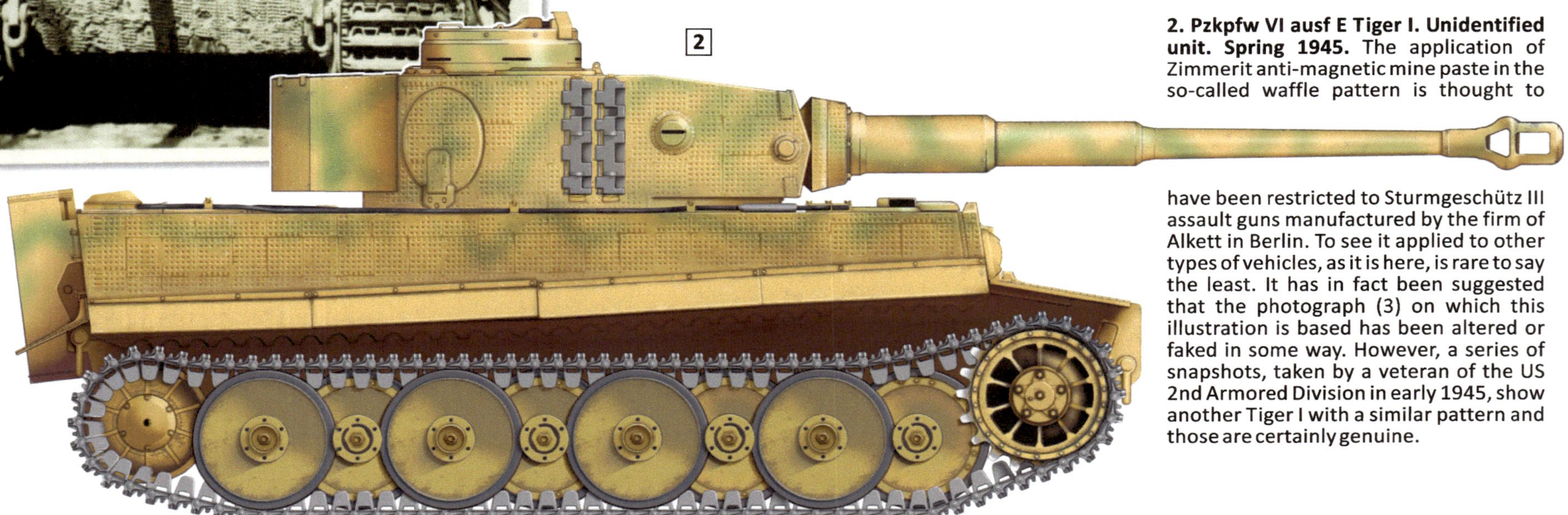

2. Pzkpfw VI ausf E Tiger I. Unidentified unit. Spring 1945. The application of Zimmerit anti-magnetic mine paste in the so-called waffle pattern is thought to have been restricted to Sturmgeschütz III assault guns manufactured by the firm of Alkett in Berlin. To see it applied to other types of vehicles, as it is here, is rare to say the least. It has in fact been suggested that the photograph (3) on which this illustration is based has been altered or faked in some way. However, a series of snapshots, taken by a veteran of the US 2nd Armored Division in early 1945, show another Tiger I with a similar pattern and those are certainly genuine.

1

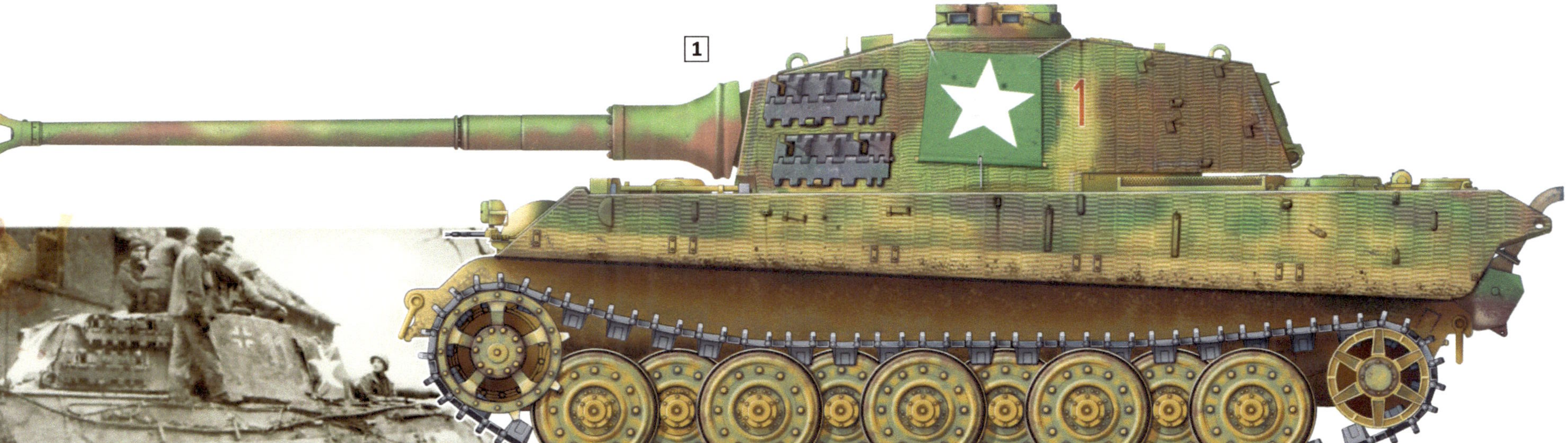

2

1. PzKpfw Tiger ausf B. 2.Kompanie, schwere Panzer-Abteilung 506. Early 1945. Captured in late 1944 and restored to running order, this tank was used for evaluation purposes well into the new year. The Allied white recognition stars were painted onto pieces of cloth and displayed on the hull glacis and on both sides and rear of the turret (2). The tank's company number of 211, in red with a white outline, is partly visible in our photograph. The chalk markings on the Schürzen warn that this vehicle may be mined.

3

3. PzKpfw Tiger ausf B. Schwere Panzer-Abteilung 506. March 1945. Photographed near Mayen, about 20 kilometres east of Koblenz, this tank may be one of the Tigers disabled in this area during the first week of March or one of the immobile tanks that provided fire support for an attack made by the infantry of 326.Volksgrenadier-Division at about the same time. Only fifty tanks were produced with these early turrets and few could have been operational by this time.The mottled camouflage is typical of the previous summer and much of the Zimmerit paste has been broken off. The only visible marking is the Balkenkreuz on the turret side.

1

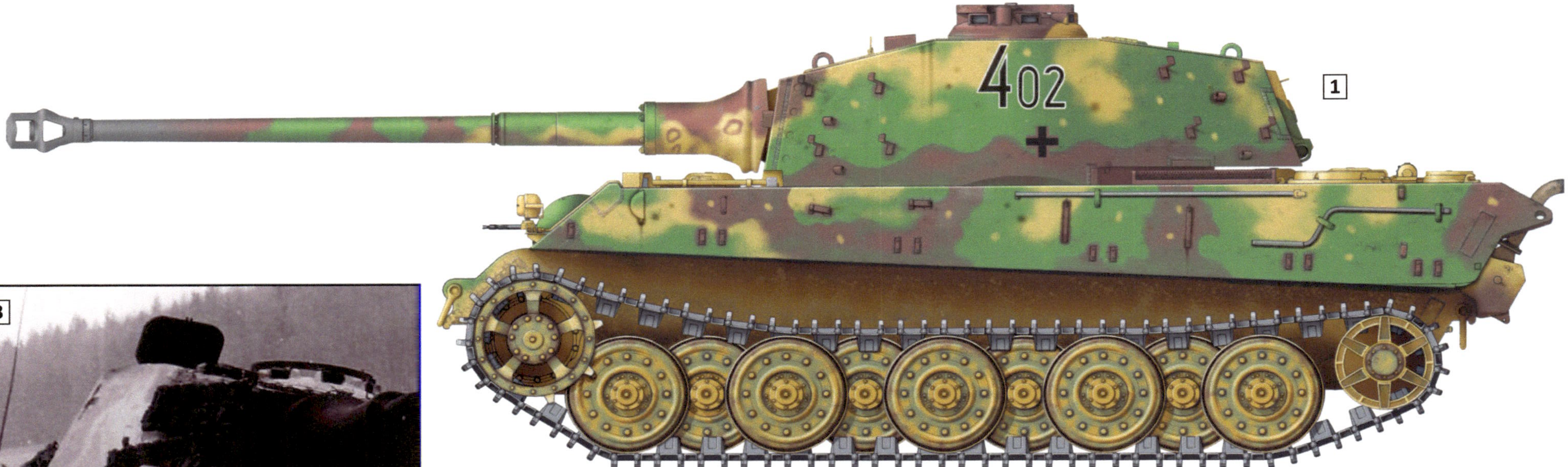

3

1. PzKpfw Tiger ausf B. 4.Kompanie, schwere Panzer-Abteilung 507. April 1945. Photographed outside Osterode, north-east of Kassel, this vehicle was probably the battalion's last operational tank. The style of turret number, where the company identifier was significantly larger than the other numbers, was a common feature of this battalion's Tigers. The use of the number 4 is not so easily explained as the battalion was rebuilt in February 1945 with two weak companies. The outline of the Balkenkreuz is an obvious dark shade in the photograph on which our illustration is based and is rendered here as Rotbraun although no definitive identification is possible. Note the 'rings' of camouflage on the gun mantlet similar to those seen on the tank depicted on page 26.

2

1. PzKpfw Tiger ausf B. Schwere Panzer-Abteilung 507. April 1945. Although the official caption of the US Signal Corps photograph of this tank states that it was taken near Osterode on 12 April 1945, the location may in fact be the road between Parensen and Harste, further to the west. This vehicle could be one of the tanks temporarily attached to SS-Regiment Holzer which took part in an attack towards Harste on 9 April when the battalion lost four Tigers. It is painted in a simplified variation of one of the factory-applied schemes which seems to be made up of just two colours. The darker shade is rendered here as Olivgrün but may possibly have been Rotbraun and the pattern can also be seen in our photograph (3). This is one of the last Tigers assembled by Henschel and is fitted with the single link track. Although it is not visible in our photograph I have assumed the presence of the last version of the drive sprocket.

1

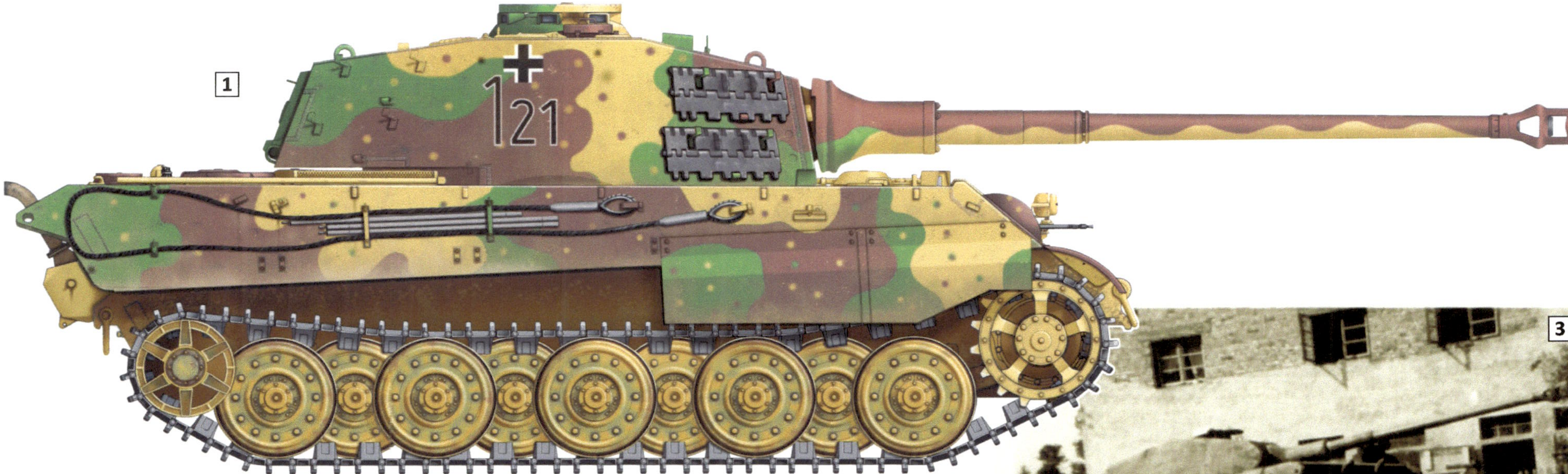

3

1. PzKpfw Tiger ausf B. 1.Kompanie, schwere Panzer-Abteilung 507. Late March 1945. Abandoned between Harste and Lenglern, west of the Göttigen to Northeim road, this tank is almost certainly one of the battalion's vehicles that were attached to SS-Panzer-Brigade Westfalen. The style of turret number, an identifying feature of this battalion, is quite clear in the photograph on which this illustration is based although 1.Kompanie reported that no tanks were on hand as late as 4 April 1945.

2

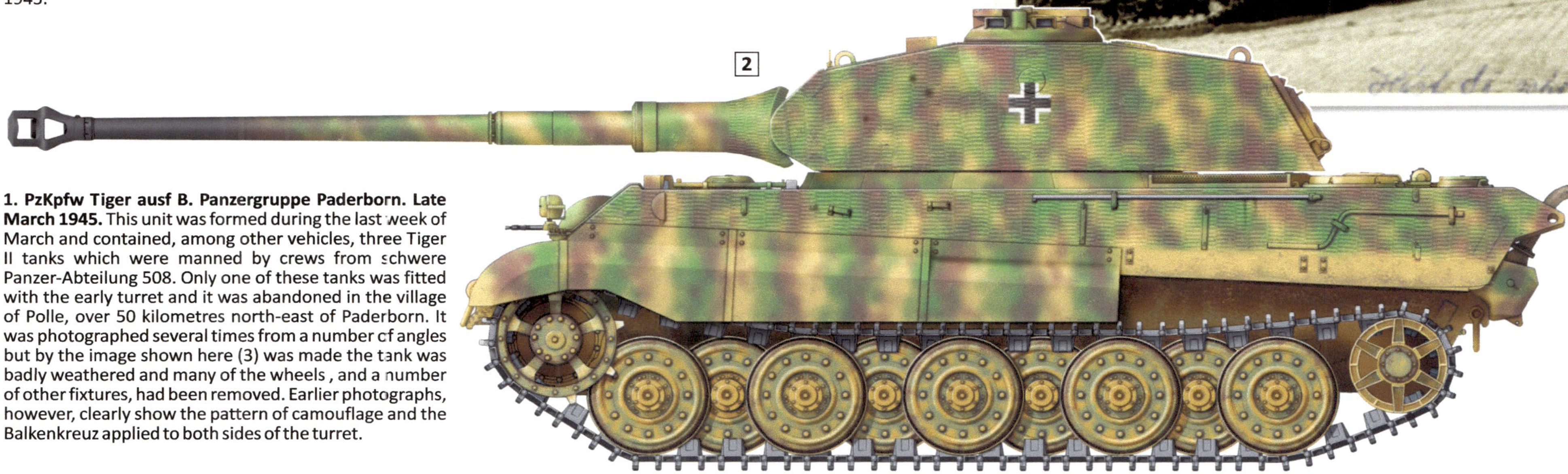

1. PzKpfw Tiger ausf B. Panzergruppe Paderborn. Late March 1945. This unit was formed during the last week of March and contained, among other vehicles, three Tiger II tanks which were manned by crews from schwere Panzer-Abteilung 508. Only one of these tanks was fitted with the early turret and it was abandoned in the village of Polle, over 50 kilometres north-east of Paderborn. It was photographed several times from a number of angles but by the image shown here (3) was made the tank was badly weathered and many of the wheels, and a number of other fixtures, had been removed. Earlier photographs, however, clearly show the pattern of camouflage and the Balkenkreuz applied to both sides of the turret.

1

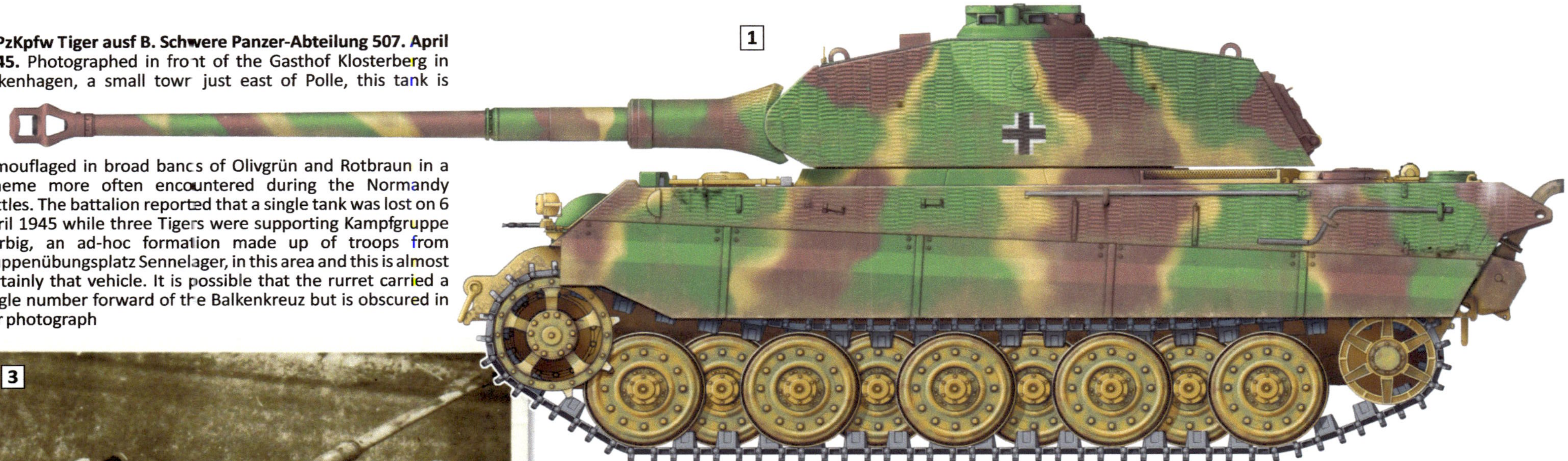

1. PzKpfw Tiger ausf B. Schwere Panzer-Abteilung 507. April 1945. Photographed in front of the Gasthof Klosterberg in Falkenhagen, a small town just east of Polle, this tank is camouflaged in broad bands of Olivgrün and Rotbraun in a scheme more often encountered during the Normandy battles. The battalion reported that a single tank was lost on 6 April 1945 while three Tigers were supporting Kampfgruppe Görbig, an ad-hoc formation made up of troops from Truppenübungsplatz Sennelager, in this area and this is almost certainly that vehicle. It is possible that the rurret carried a single number forward of the Balkenkreuz but is obscured in our photograph

3

2

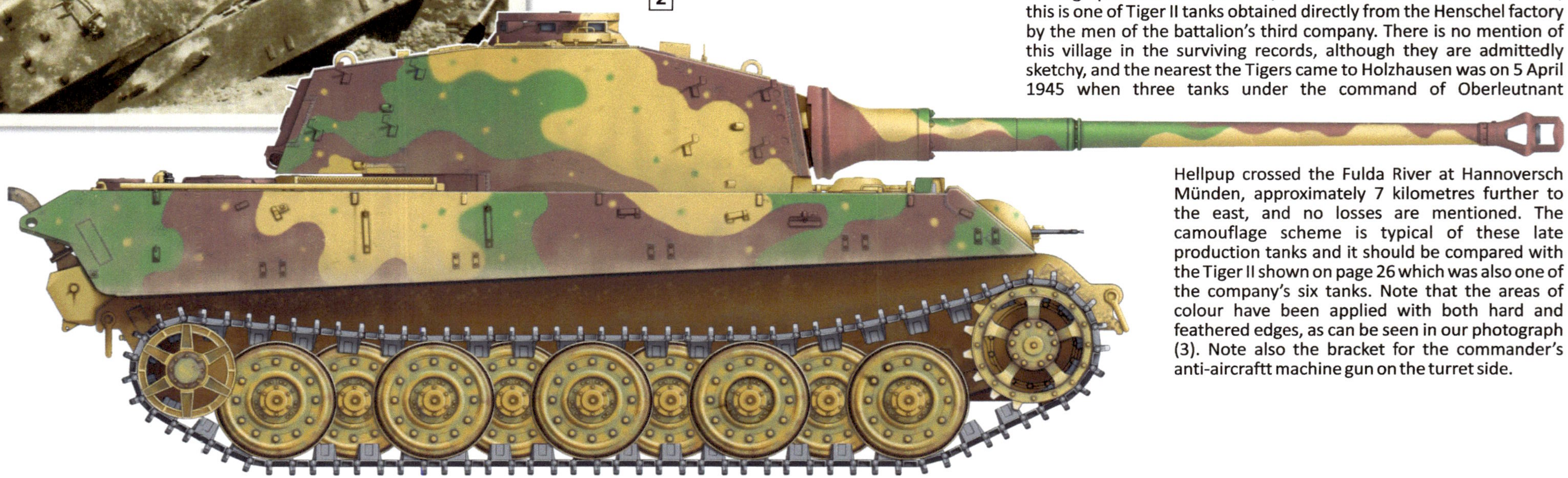

2. PzKpfw Tiger ausf B. Schwere Panzer-Abteilung 510. April 1945. Photographed near Holzhausen, about 10 Kilometres north of Kassel, this is one of Tiger II tanks obtained directly from the Henschel factory by the men of the battalion's third company. There is no mention of this village in the surviving records, although they are admittedly sketchy, and the nearest the Tigers came to Holzhausen was on 5 April 1945 when three tanks under the command of Oberleutnant Hellpup crossed the Fulda River at Hannoversch Münden, approximately 7 kilometres further to the east, and no losses are mentioned. The camouflage scheme is typical of these late production tanks and it should be compared with the Tiger II shown on page 26 which was also one of the company's six tanks. Note that the areas of colour have been applied with both hard and feathered edges, as can be seen in our photograph (3). Note also the bracket for the commander's anti-aircraftt machine gun on the turret side.

PzKpfw Tiger ausf B. 3.Kompanie, schwere Panzer-Abteilung 510. April 1945. Said to have been photographed in Rengershausen this vehicle is one of the six Tiger II tanks picked-up from the Henschel factory at Kassel by crews from the battalion's 3.Kompanie on 29 March 1945. According to the best evidence we have, the tanks initially moved south-west to take part in the defence of Fritzlar and then withdrew through Kassel towards the north-east and the crossing of the Fulda at Hannoversch Münden. The town of Rengershausen is over 30 kilometres from Fritzlar, on the other side of the Kellerwald-Edersee forest, and the tank may have been moved to the town by its captors. Indeed, at least one image shows this Tiger in an open field and this tank may have been lost as early as 2 April. In any case it was photographed from several angles allowing this representation of the camouflage pattern. Note that in all the available photographs it is fitted with the narrow transport tracks.

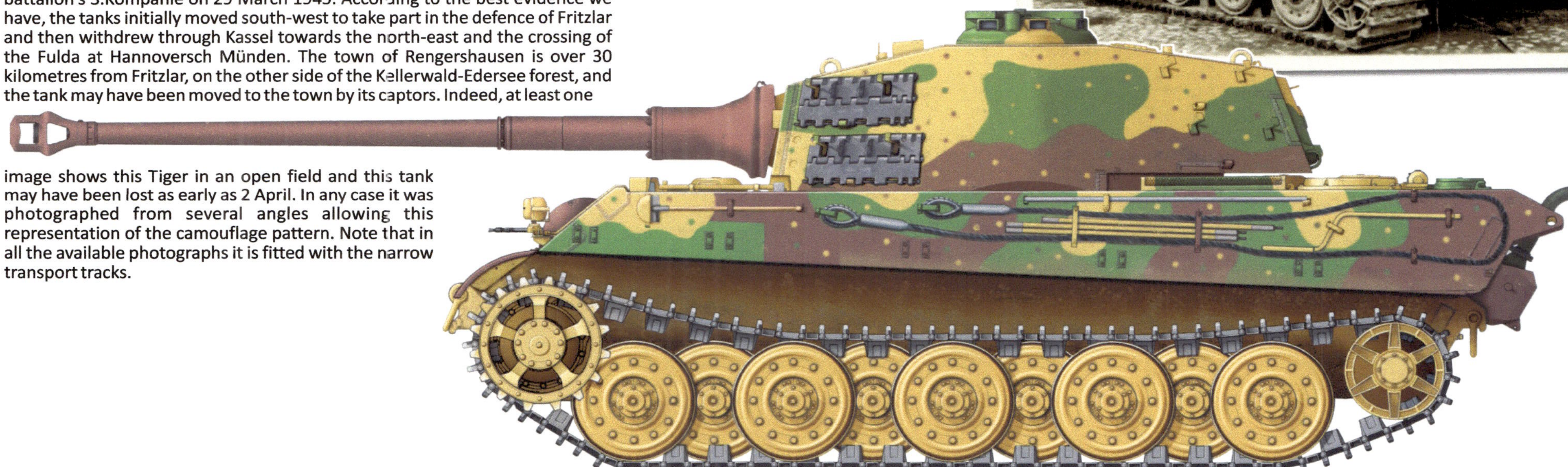

PzKpfw Tiger ausf B. Schwere Panzer-Abteilung 511. April 1945. Thought to have been disabled on 5 April in a firefight with US Army tank destroyers, this vehicle is one of the eight Tiger II tanks taken over by the crews of the battalion's 3.Kompanie directly from the Henschel factory on 31 March 1945. The location has been confirmed as the autobahn overpass at Heiligenrode, today a suburb of Kassel. Although this tank was photographed numerous times from different angles, a truly accurate rendering of the camouflage scheme is not possible due to the significant damage and wear which is evident from our photograph at right. Commonly referred to today as the 'Octopus Scheme' the pattern is highly unusual and may be unique, although it is in some ways similar to the camouflage applied to the Tiger of schwere Panzer-Abteilung 507 depicted in figure 2 on page 22. Although there is no way to be certain, it does seem likely that this tank would have been fitted with both sets of hull Schürzen before it left the factory. In every known photograph this tank is fitted with the narrow transport tracks rendered here. It should be mentioned that the white swastika shown in our photograph is a post-war addition.

TIGER I

TIGERGRUPPE FEHRMANN

GERMANY, SPRING 1945

1/72 SCALE

STEVE SHRIMPTON

British modeller Steve Shrimpton's 1/72 scale replica is based on the Dragon Models Tiger I and depicts a hybrid Tiger I with an early production turret and late production hull, complete with steel road wheels. Photo-etched brass details and a turned aluminium barrel with a brass muzzle brake were also used to replace some of the kit parts. There are numerous theories regarding the possible colours applied to the Tigers of Oberleutnant Fehrmann's command, however, all are based on the interpretation of black and white photographs where the tanks have been damaged and Steve's decision to apply a worn camouflage based on a Dunkelgelb RAL 7028 base coat is equally valid.

Steve's model depicts Tiger F13, commanded by Feldwebel Bellof, as it was being prepared for battle, without the damage so obvious in the available period photographs of this tank. At top, the turret and hull with camouflage and markings applied prior to weathering. Above and at right, a crew member hastily applies the tank's number.

TIGER II

3.KOMPANIE, SCHWERE SS-PANZER-ABTEILUNG 501

BELGIUM, LATE 1944

1/35 SCALE

LESTER PLASKITT

Many readers will be familiar with the outstanding models produced by Lester Plaskitt and the ultra-realistec effects shown here are typical of his work. Below, the basic camouflage pattern applied to the entire tank and the turret number handpainted in the distinctive blue and yellow of the battalion's third company. The images at the bottom of the page show the early stages of the weathering process.

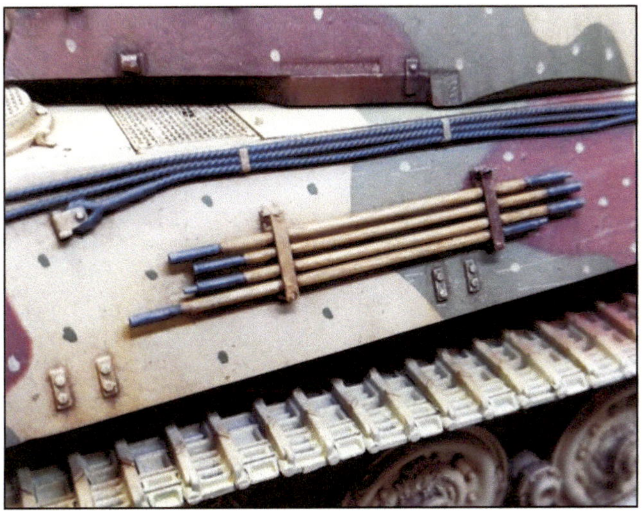

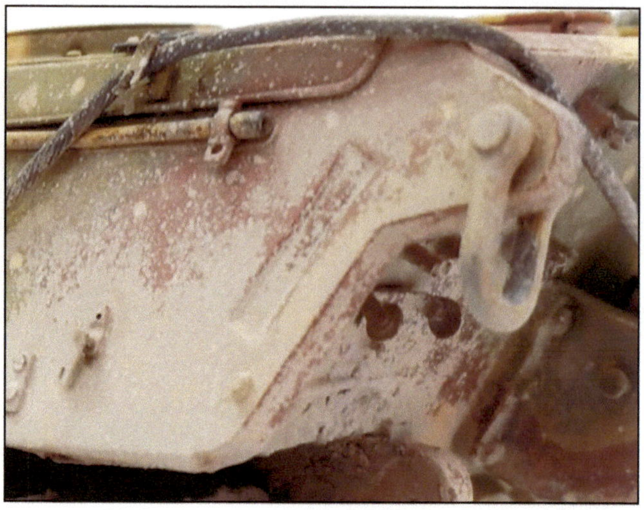

The finished model showing extensive weathering and wear. Much of the chipping to the metal surfaces was painstakingly applied with a fine brush and as many modellers will be aware, these effects are all too easy to overdo.

The attention to detail is shown to good effect in these photographs of the completed model. Lester used a number of different pigments in the painting and weathering of this kit including Acrylicos Vallejo and AK Interactive. The extremely realistic tracks are the plastic version supplied with the Meng kit.

TIGER II

SCHWERE PANZER-ABTEILUNG 506

GERMANY, SPRING 1945

1/35 SCALE

SHENG HUI

Chinese modeller Sheng Hui is actually the proprietor of ROCHM Model and the creator of the company's large range of photo-etched and resin detail sets for 1/35 scale kits. All the details used to create this replica were taken from ROCHM's range and some are shown below including: 1.The engine intake grills and fire extinguisher. 2. The front fender with its hinges. 3 and 4. The clamps for the exhaust and towing clevises. 5. The tool brackets and fittings for the hull Schürzen. 6. The rear mudguard with finely detailed hinge and clamp. This company's offerings are also discussed in the Modelling Products section of this book which begins on page 37.

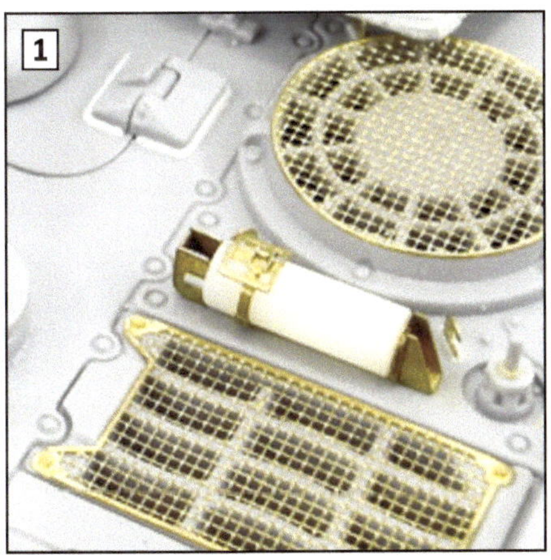

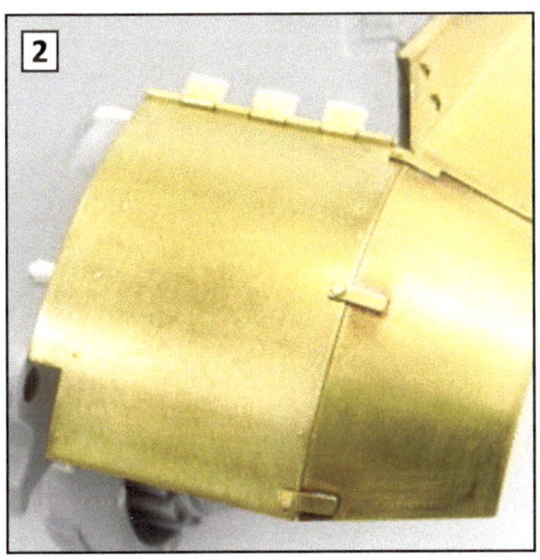

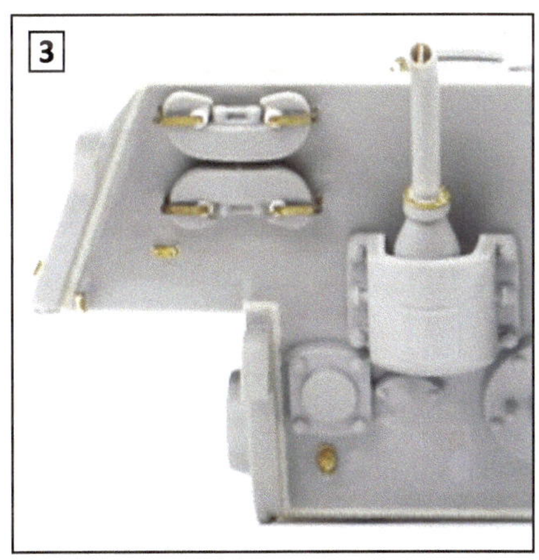

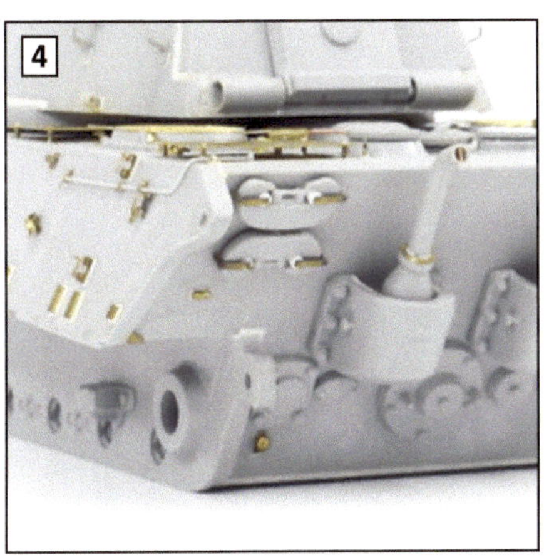

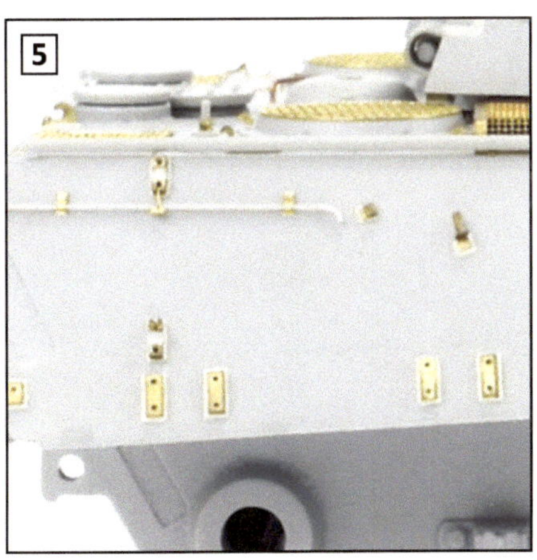

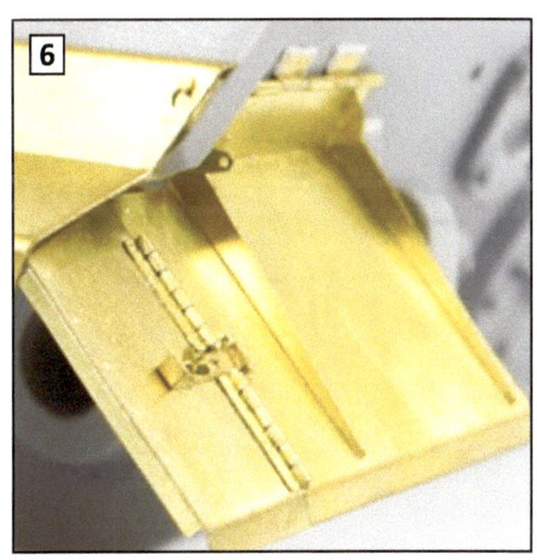

Sheng Hui's completed model painted as a the Tiger II of the battalion's first company which was disabled and abandoned near Burg Reuland, south of St Vith, during the fighting in the Ardennes. As can be seen from the photograph on the previous page the coating of Zimmerit was labouriously applied by hand by layering modelling putty on the kit's horizontal surfaces and the scoring the putty with a small screwdriver. The tracks, made up of individual metal links, retain their realistic appearance even after extensive painting and weathering.

To say that the Tiger tank is a perennial favourite among armour modellers would be something of an understatement. Scale replicas of these deservedly famous tanks have been produced by every major manufacturer, and many minor and less well known companies, since the early 1960s when the first plastic construction kits were released. Although the early products would today be considered little more than toys, the more recent models are highly detailed representations, increasingly featuring photo-etched brass parts, turned aluminium barrels and workable tracks as standard, often depicting variants which were operational for just a short period of time or which may have only taken part in a single battle. The expansion of the market in recent years has also contributed to the proliferation of smaller, specialised companies producing accessories in resin, photo-etched metal, plastic, wood and other materials allowing a level of super-detailing which had previously been the province of a few master modellers. Models of the Tiger are produced in a number of scales from tiny 6mm wargames miniatures to the huge, radio-controlled 1/6 scale versions but these are at the extreme ends of the market and I have chosen to concentrate on the most popular modelling scales of 1/35, 1/48 and 1/72. I should mention that this list is far from exhaustive, mostly due to reasons of space, and to compensate I have omitted some companies that were mentioned in the first volume in the TankCraft series, *Tiger I and Tiger II Tanks, German Army and Waffen-SS, Eastern Front 1944,* and included a number that could not be accommodated in that book. In addition, I have limited any comment or critique of these kits or products to those of which I have firsthand knowledge.

An index of manufacturers and their contact details can be found on page 64.

TAMIYA INCORPORATED

This Japanese company, which began life as a sawmill, has been manufacturing plastic kits since 1959, releasing their first armour model, two years later. By the early 1970s Tamiya was producing a large range of armoured vehicles and accessories and the company was almost solely responsible for the rise in popularity of 1/35 scale. Like Airfix, the adoption of a constant scale proved popular at a time when many manufacturers were making models to fit the box in which they would eventually be marketed. Tamiya's early kits were, for their day, highly detailed relatively easy to assemble and, most importantly, affordable. From 2003 Tamiya began releasing a series of armour models in 1/48 scale, including early and late models of the Tiger I and a Tiger II, and this line has been extremely successful for the company. At the time of writing Tamiya produces, in 1/35 scale, early, mid-production and late versions of the Tiger I, a Tiger II fitted with the Production turret and coated with Zimmerit , a later Tiger II without the Zimmerit and a Tiger II with the earlier Porsche turret. Radio-controlled models of an early production Tiger I and a Tiger II are produced in both 1/35 and 1/16 scale.

Tamiya's 1/35 scale Tiger II with Production turret marketed as Königstiger Einsatz-Kommando Ardennes.

Below, 1. Tracks and steel roadwheels from the 1/48 scale late production Tiger I. 2. Detail of the mid production Tiger I kit in 1/35 scale. 3. Tamiya also sells sheets of Zimmerit texture For the Tiger I and Tiger II.

1

2

3

TRUMPETER/HOBBY BOSS

Often thought to be separate entities, these Chinese companies are in fact owned by the same corporation, are located at the same address and are essentially the same firm although different models are marketed separately under the two labels. Hobby Boss produces a 1/16 scale mid-production Tiger I while Trumpeter's range is far more extensive encompassing a number of 1/72 scale models and a 1/16 scale Tiger II which can be built with either the Production or earlier Porsche turret. There are also options of other late or early production features.

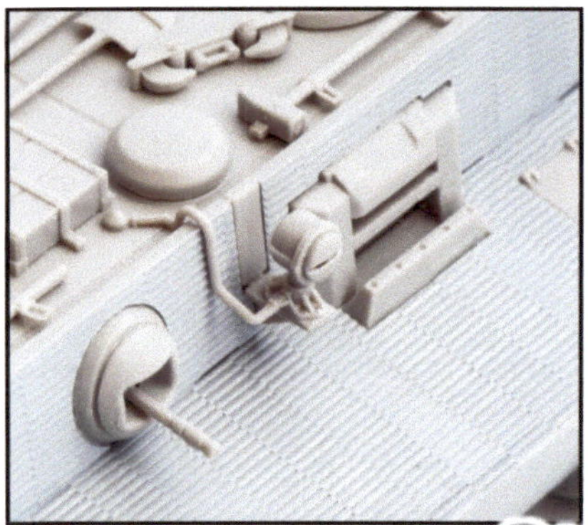

Below: The Hobby Boss 1/16 scale mid production Tiger I. This model comes assembled and pre-painted in the scheme shown here. At left, 1. Detail of the 1/35 scale mid production Tiger I with Zimmerit fitted. 2. The optional turrets for the 1/35 scale Tiger II

ACADEMY

Based in Korea, this company's Military Miniatures range of 1/35 scale figures and vehicles includes an early and mid production Tiger I, a late production version and a Hybrid model with later steel wheels, optional Zimmerit texture for the hull and turret, early drum-style commander's cupola and a selection of markings marketed as Tiger I Hybrid Gruppe Fehrmann referring to the six Tigers from Panzerschule 1 Bergen which were commanded by Oberleutnant Rudolf Fehrmann during the last days of the war. Most of these models have been repackaged at some time, often with only minor changes or new markings, although some include additional parts.

Below: Academy's late production Tiger I kit in 1/35 scale built with photo-etched brass details from Eduard Model Accessories. Note that the model does not have Zimmerit although most, if not all, these tanks would have had the paste applied before leaving the assembly plant. The images at left show the detailed interior of the early production model.

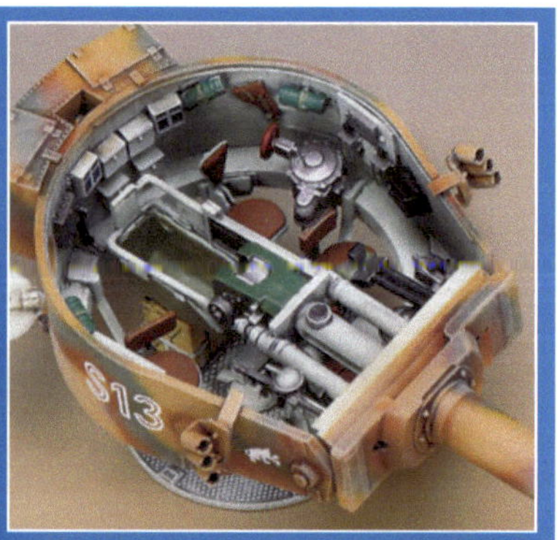

DRAGON MODELS LIMITED

At the time of writing this Hong Kong based company's catalogue contained over forty models of Tiger I and II variants in 1/35 and 1/72 scale including kits of the Bergetiger recovery vehicle. That number does not include the Jagdtiger tank destroyer and Sturmtiger assault gun, both offered in different scales. The larger scale models include early, mid and late production tanks as well as the Tiger I hybrid version. From time to time many of these models are repackaged with bonus items such as photo-etched parts or new sets of markings under the Cyberhobby label. Dragon also offers a number of the same tanks, pre-painted and assembled, in 1/144 scale and a complete range of 1/72 scale tanks, again pre-painted and assembled. To complement the vehicles there is a large range of highly detailed, plastic multi-pose figures.

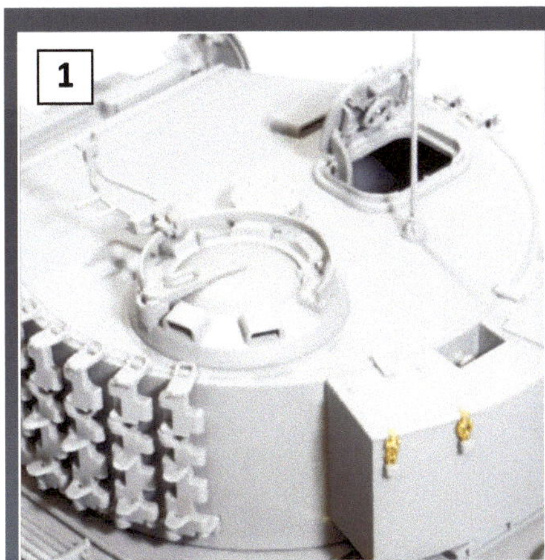

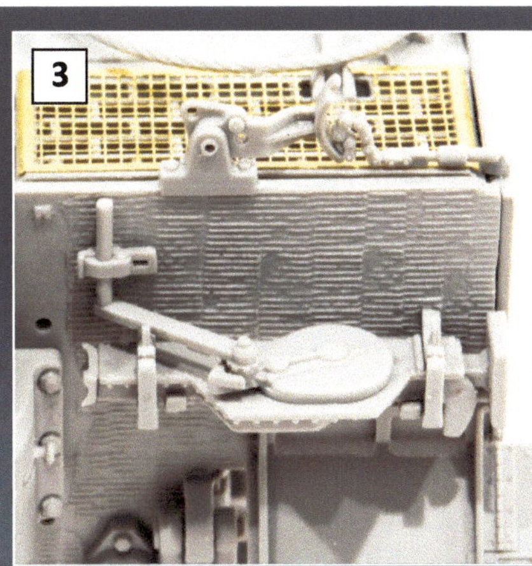

Above, 1. Dragon Models' mid production Befehlspanzer command tank in 1/35 scale. 2 and 3. Details of the 1/35 scale late production Tiger I model showing the jack attached to the rear hull and the photo-etched brass parts that are included in the kit.

At left: Dragon Models 1/35 scale Tiger II with Production turret built and painted by Japanese company Platz Hobby. Below, 4. The 1/72 scale late production Tiger I model completed with photo-etched details from E.T. Model. 5 and 6. Details of Dragon's 1/35 scale Tiger II variously marketed as late production, Ardennes or Battle of the Bulge Tiger.

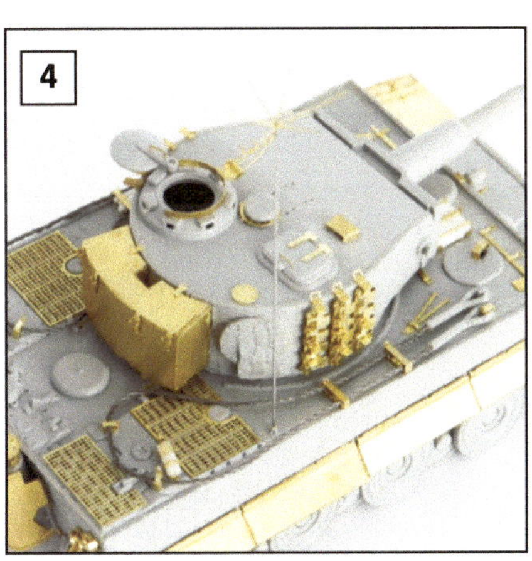

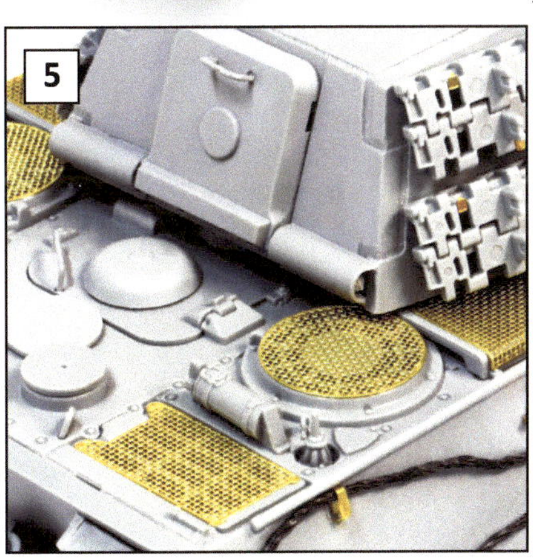

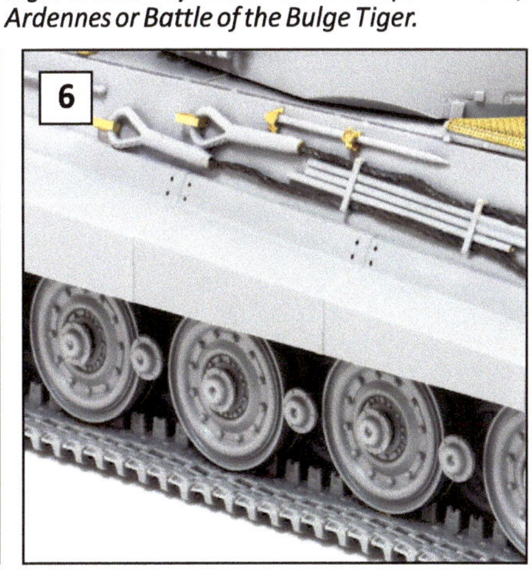

HOBBY FAN/AFV CLUB

Hobby Fan Enterprises is the parent company of the better known AFV Club, both of which are based in Taiwan. The current AFV Club catalogue includes a Tiger I early production model and a late production version fitted with narrow transport tracks, both in 1/35 scale. The company also offers, in 1/48 scale, an early production vehicle and a Tiger I marketed both as a 'final' and 'latest' production model. The latter features some of the last modifications incorporated into production including the 40mm turret roof, later-style loader's hatch with a fully Revised engine deck and tool placement. Most AFV Club kits include non-standard items such as turned metal gun barrels, photo-etched brass parts and a sheet of water-slide transfers offering numerous schemes. The company also provides solid plastic and workable tracks in individual links in both 1/35 and 1/48 scale in addition to ammunition, wooden crates and other general items. The 1/48 scale late production Tiger I model formally produced by Skybow is now marketed under the AFV Club logo.

Below: The AFV Club late production Tiger I in transport mode. This kit is essentially the same as the company's Tiger I Latest Model and Tiger I Late Model Michael Wittman Special with the some different parts. At right: The 1/48 scale Tiger I late production kit, formerly marketed by Sky Bow and the workable plastic transport tracks.

ZVEZDA

Founded in 1990, this Russian company has grown to become one of the country's larger exporters. In recent years Zvezda's catalogue has become heavily weighted towards modern Russian and Soviet-era vehicle and aircraft models but does include an early production model Tiger I in 1/35 scale which is a retooling of an older kit first released in 1996. The same version is also offered in 1/72 and 1/100 scale. More recent releases include a Tiger II with the Porsche turret and Zimmerit and a later Tiger II with the Production turret without Zimmerit, both reworkings of Dragon kits with new, added parts. The long awaited 1/72 scale version of the Tiger II is among the company's latest releases.

Above: Zvezda's 1/35 scale Tiger with Production, or as listed her, Henschel turret. Rather confusingly the same, or very similar, box art is sometimes used for different scales. At right: The 1/35 scale early production Tiger I built with photo-etched parts from Eduard Model Accessories.

RYE FIELD MODELS

Based in Hong Kong, this company released three kits depicting Tiger I variants all in the short space of time between September 2015 and February 2016. An initial production model depicts a Tiger with the modifications seen on the first tanks sent to Tunisia and the mid production version features extensive interior detailing. The third release, depicting a hybrid Tiger I of Tigergruppe Fehrmann, utilises parts from the earlier kits. The late production Tiger I kit which was scheduled to be released in May 2018 was still listed as a future release at the time of writing, some two months later. These are not re-worked or re-issued kits but completely new models.

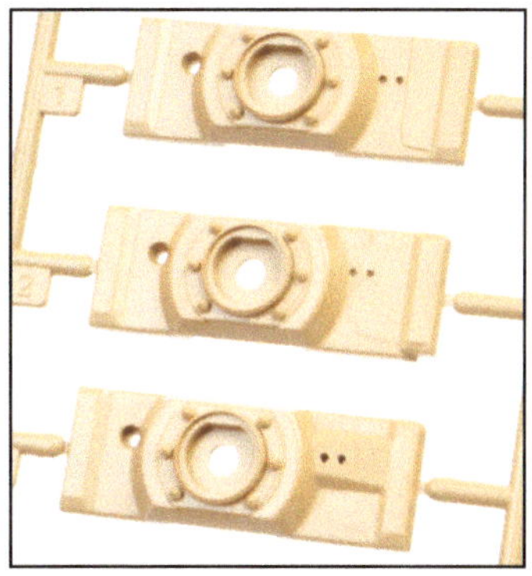

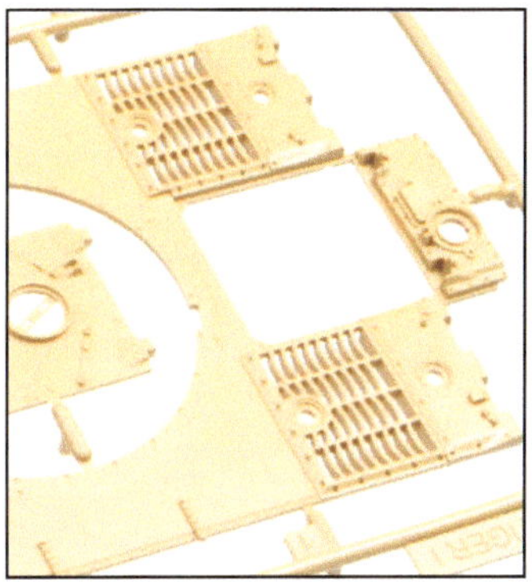

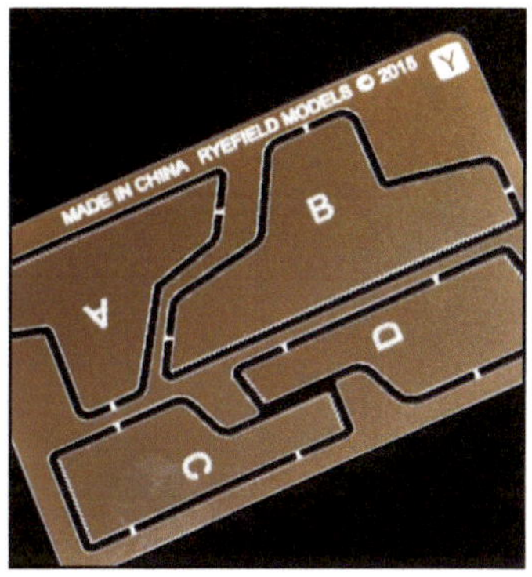

Above: The box art for Rye Field Model's late production Tiger I. Eagerly awaited, this kit will probably be available by the time this book is released. At right, 1. The drive sprocket and tracks of the Tiger I early production kit. 2. Optional gun mantlets in 1/35 scale from the Gruppe Fehrmann model. 3. The rear deck of the early production model. 4. The Zimmerit tool that is included with the Tiger I hybrid kit. I should mention that the putty necessary to create the Zimmerit coating is not included with the kit.

TAKOM

This is one of the newest model manufacturers, setting up shop in Hong Kong in 2013 as Takom World and shortly afterwards expanding to open a plant in mainland China where the models are actually produced. Most kits are in 1/35 scale and the company offers models of the Tiger II with the Porsche and Production turrets and a complete set of individual track links. The Tiger models are both marketed in two versions, one with parts for extensive interior detailing as shown here. The latter also includes photo-etched brass parts including an incredibly detailed set of 88mm rounds with appropriate notations stamped into the base of each.

Above and at right: Parts from Takom's 1/35 scale Tiger II kit including the extensive interior details.

ITALERI

This Italian company has been producing plastic models since its foundation in 1962 and the current catalogue contains Tiger I models depicting early, mid and late production versions and a recently-added late war Hybrid model in 1/35 scale. In 1/72 scale Italeri offers a Tiger II with the Production turret, originally manufactured by ESCI and was first released in 1974, and a late production Tiger I in their Fast Assembly range, a very basic kit comprising just ten pieces each. of the large model manufacturers Italeri alone has ventured into 1/56 scale with a Tiger I late production kit and a model of the Tiger II which contains both the Porsche and Henschel turrets. This scale complements 28mm wargames figures of which there are now quite a number on the market.

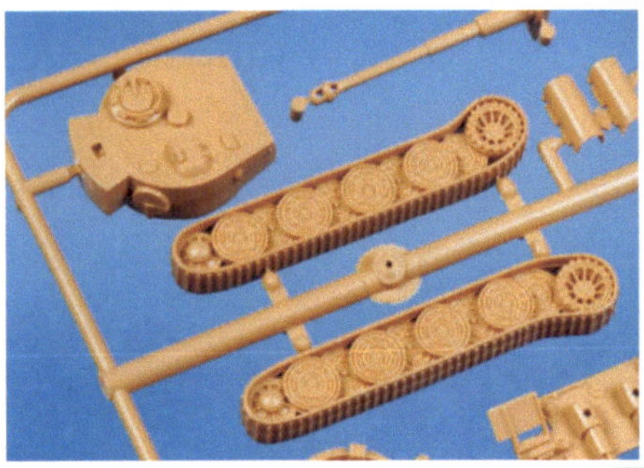

Below: Italeri's mid production Tiger I kit in 1/35 scale built with Hauler's photo-etched brass details.

At left: Italeri's 1/56 scale kits with the box art for the Tiger II and parts form the late production Tiger I kit.

REVELL AND AIRFIX

No listing of model replicas of the Tiger tank would be complete without some mention of the venerable Airfix kit. First released in 1964, the packaging and box art has changed many times over the intervening years, as has the ownership of the company, although the model itself has remained unaltered. Wildly inaccurate with ill-fitting parts and tracks that could only be described as rudimentary it was, however, the starting point for many of today's great armour modellers and remains a sentimental favourite. The company's Tiger II in 1/76 scale is a reasonably good kit although it cannot be compared to the offerings from Dragon and Revell. The latter's 1/72 scale PzKpfw VI Ausf H kit was first released in 1997 and since that time it has been re-boxed several times and updated with extra parts, including the cast cupola and steel road wheels to produce the PzKpfw VI Ausf E version. Both these kits featured realistic link and length tracks and were the first accurate renditions of this important tank in the smaller scales. Readers should note that although the box art of the most recently released models depict a vehicle coated with Zimmerit, as most of the mid and late production tanks were, this is not included with the kit.

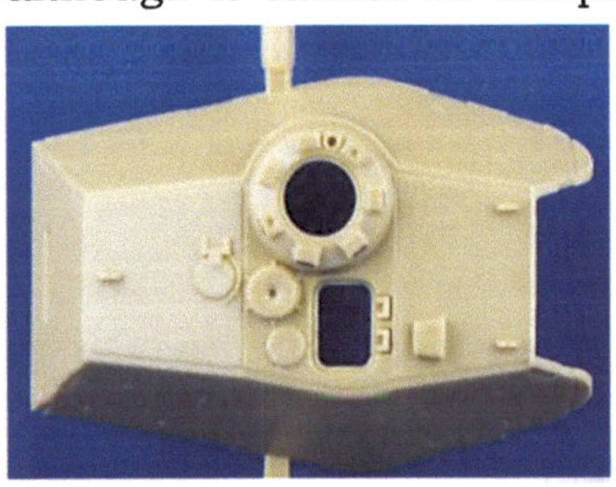

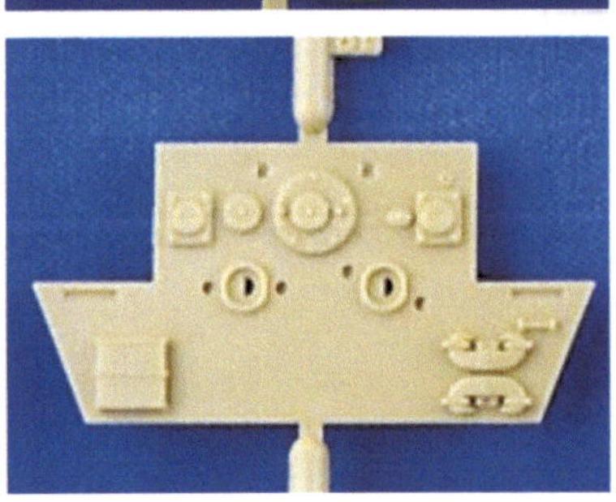

Below: The Airfix 1/76 scale Tiger II built and painted for the company's catalogue. Note that most of the hull details, including the towing cables, are moulded on unlike the Revell kit, shown at left, or the Dragon Models' offering. Note also that most of these early production tanks would have been coated with Zimmerit.

MENG-MODEL

Founded in 2011 this Chinese company largely specialises in modern armour but has recently released a Tiger II in 1/35 scale to very favourable reviews. Well known modeller David Parker apparently advised the company during the development of the model and the box art was created by the legendary Masami Onishi who is responsible for the dramatic paintings that accompany many of Tamiya's models. The box also carries the logo of the Bovington Tank Museum Implying their cooperation although I have been unable to confirm this. I should mention that a visit to the company's web site, as with many Chinese model manufacturers, can be an exercise in frustration with the products listed here under the names of various dinosaurs. Shown here is the Meng-Model Tiger II with Production turret and below that at 1. The Zimmerit texture that accompanies the Tiger II kits. 2. A detail of the turret interior. 3. A detail of the front fender.

1

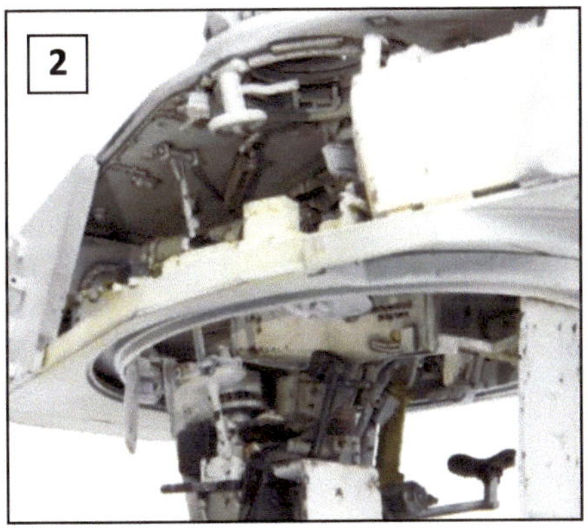

2

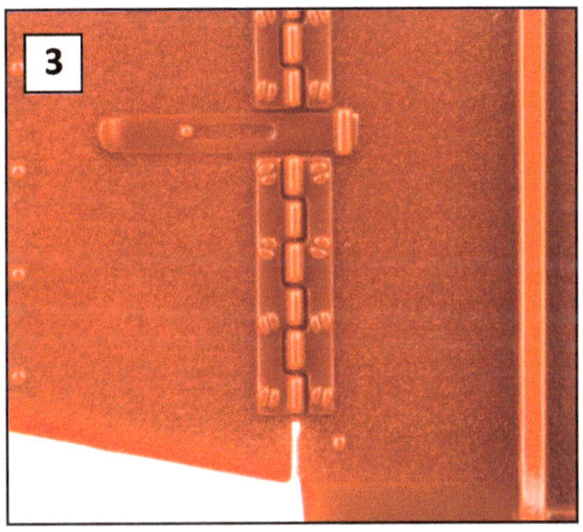

3

GRIFFON MODEL

Based in China this company produces a large range of photo-etched brass sets for the Tiger I and Tiger II in 1/35 scale to fit most manufacturers kit, although they do recommend Tamiya and Dragon. These sets are of a very high quality and usually include a large number of separate pieces. Shown below are 1. Parts for the Tiger II including the interior of the turret rear access door, the engine grills and brackets for the fire extinguisher here fitted to the Dragon Models kit. 2. Exhaust manifold covers and rear mud guards and various clamps and brackets for the mid or late production Tiger I. 3. A full photo etched brass detail set for the mid or late production Tiger I. This set also contains aluminium track pins for the spare tracks and a metal wire towing cable.

1

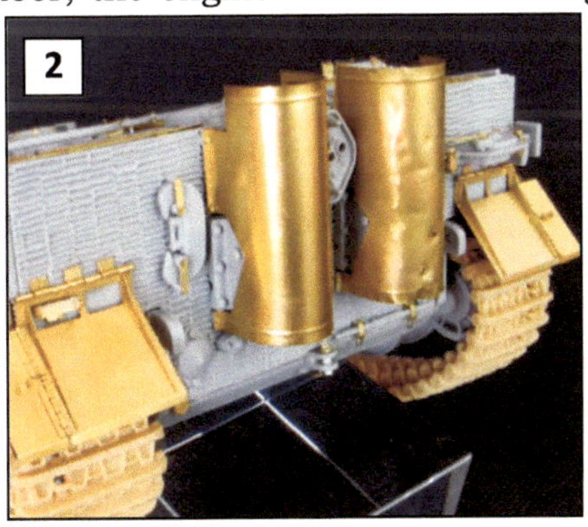

2

3

EDUARD MODEL ACCESSORIES

This Polish company has been manufacturing high-quality accessories in photo-etched brass and resin for many years and was one of the earliest firms to offer upgrade sets in the smaller scales. In addition to the upgrade sets Eduard offers complete kits of the Tiger II which are actually the Academy 1/35 scale kit with Eduard's detail sets, paint masks and markings.

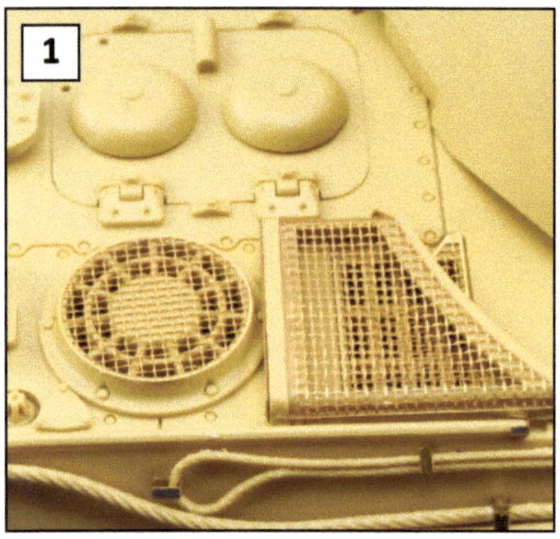

Above, 1. Details of the upgrade set for Tamyia's 1/35 scale Tiger II. 2. A section of the brass Zimmerit sheets applied to the Tamiya 1/48 scale Tiger II with Production turret. 3. Photo-etched brass details for the AFV Club 1/35 scale late production Tiger I. Below, 5. Parts from Eduard's upgrade set for the Dragon 1/72 scale Tiger I, shown here applied to the late production kit. 5. The Academy 1/35 scale late production Tiger I built with metal exhaust shrouds and rear fenders in 1/35 scale. 6. Parts from the detail set for the Zvezda 1/35 scale early production Tiger I.

The Dragon Models 1/35 scale mid production Tiger I built with Eduard's upgrade set in photo-etched brass. Not visible here are the details for the interior of the engine bay.

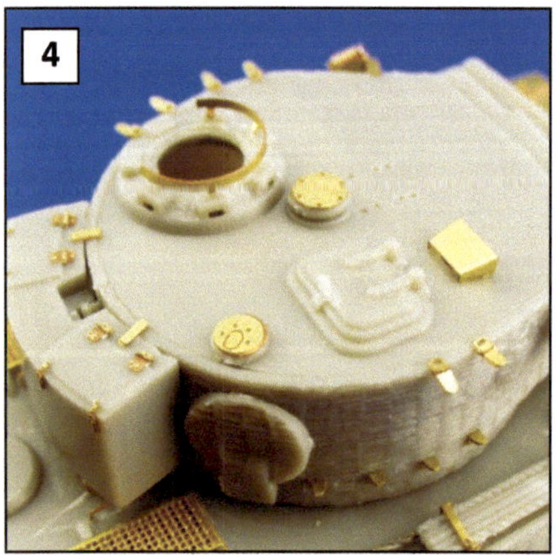

ROCHM MODEL

This company is owned and managed by master modeller Sheng Hui whose work has appeared in a number of books in the TankCraft series, including this volume. Initially specialising in 1/35 scale detail sets in resin, photo-etched brass and aluminium for the Tiger I, the company moved onto the Tiger II series and produced extensive upgrades primarily intended for the Meng, Dragon and Zvezda models, although many of the parts would of course be suitable for most 1/35 scale kits. Rochm Model's products offer exceptional detail and considering the quality, are reasonably priced. Detail sets in 1/48 and 1/72 scale are currently in the planning stage.

At left and below: Rochm's extensive detail set applied to the Meng 1/35 scale Tiger II kit. These sets are produced in super-detail and basic versions, the latter considerably cheaper and containing less parts.

Below, all in 1/35 scale: 1. Tiger I hatch interior. 2. Tiger I front fender. 3. Tiger II late style fender. 4. MG cupola mount. 5. Tiger II turret roof detail. 6. Final production Tiger II rear hull.

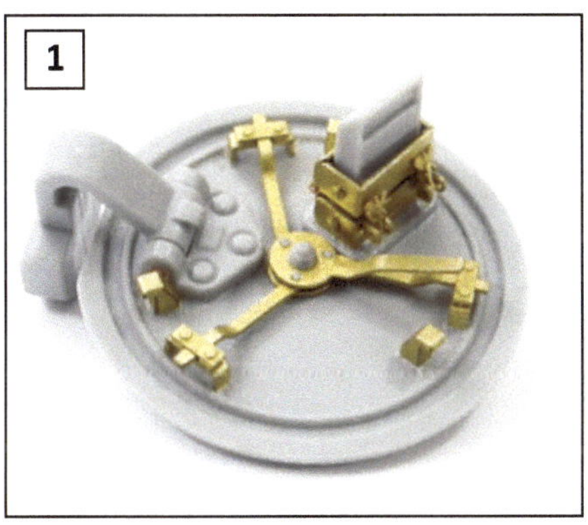

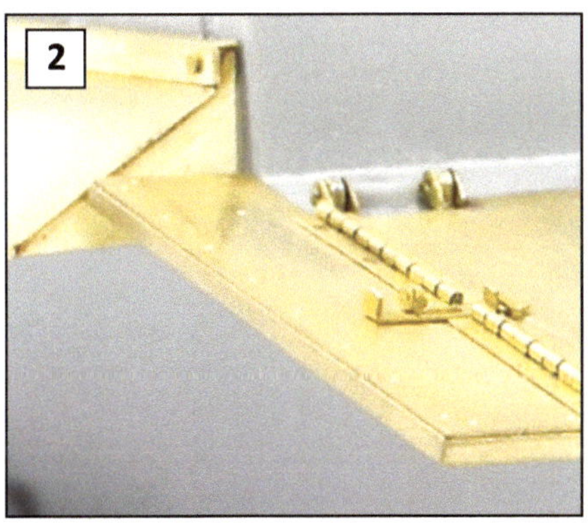

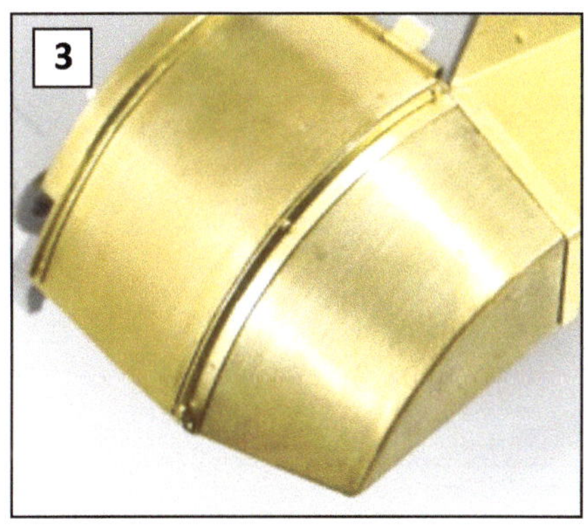

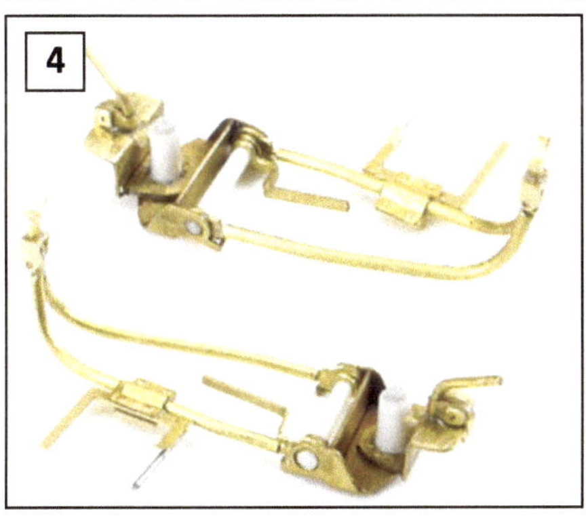

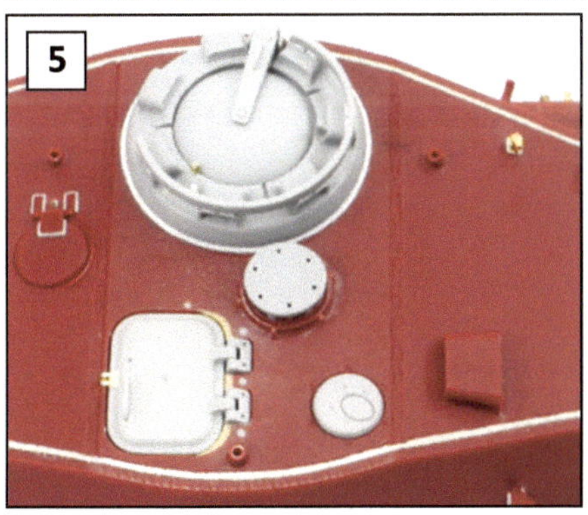

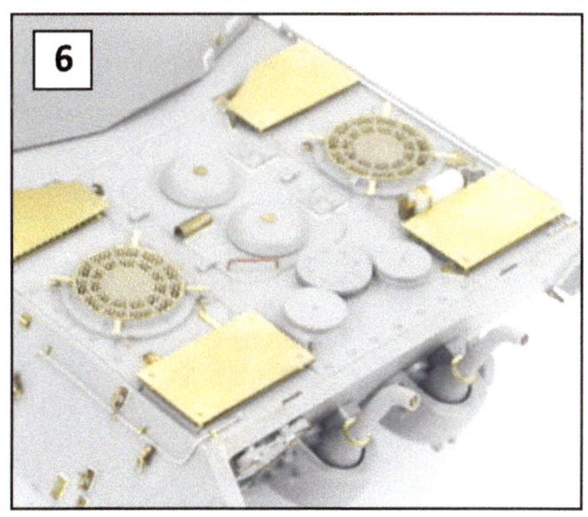

ROYAL MODEL

This Italian company has been producing high quality accessories and aftermarket parts since the early 1990s under the guidance of its founder, Roberto Reale. The catalogue includes complete upgrade sets in 1/35 scale for the early, mid and late production Tiger I and for the Tiger II. Royal Model also market a limited number of sets in 1/72 and 1/48 scale and crew figures for the larger scale models. Shown here are 1. The Tamiya Tiger I built with Royal Model photo-etched brass parts. 2. The Tiger II Kugelblende MG mount in resin. 3. Photo-etched brass parts for a 1/35 scale Tiger II.

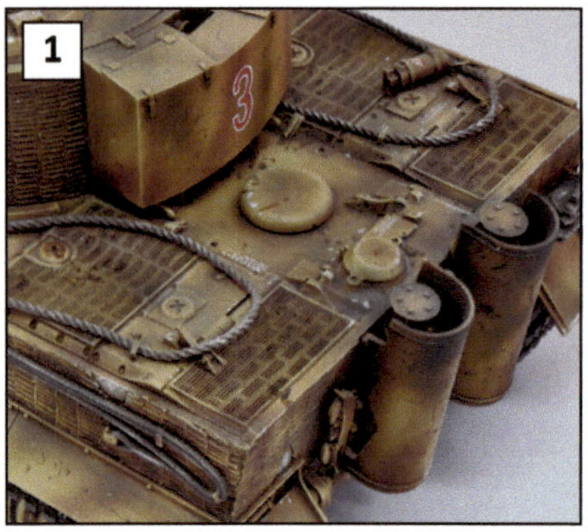

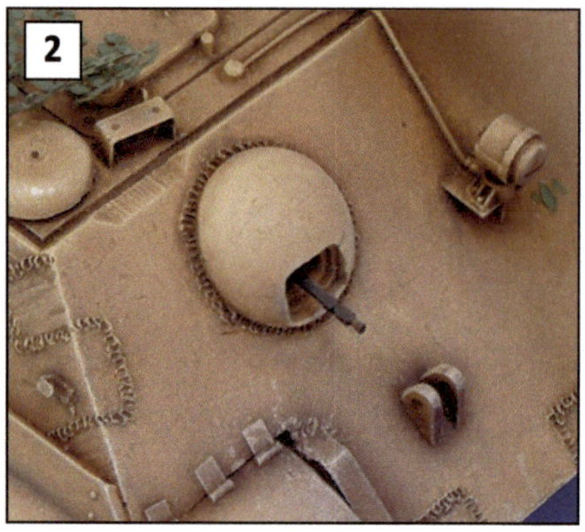

HAULER

Based in the Czech Republic, this company produces accessory sets in photo-etched brass and resin in 1/48, 1/35 and even 1/87 scale, a size which complements HO scale railway models. A number of items in the company's extensive range are now produced under the Bren Gun logo.

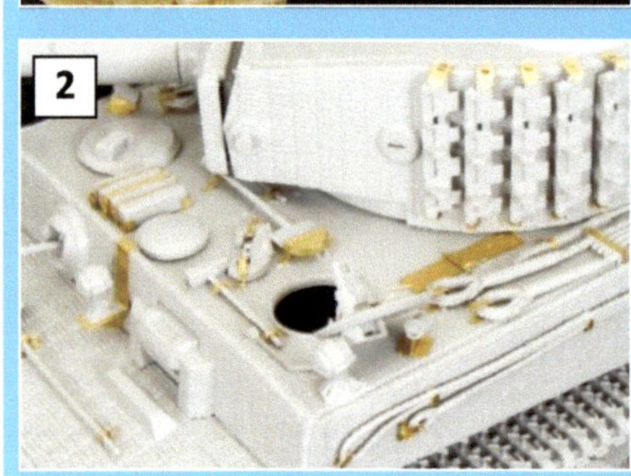

1. Hauler's photo-etched brass detail set for the Revell 1/72 scale Tiger II. 2. A generic set for 1/35 scale Tiger I models featuring parts for early, mid and late production versions.

Below: Hauler's photo-etched brass set for the Sky Bow 1/48 scale late production Tiger I, now produced by AFV Club.

VOYAGER MODEL

Voyager have been manufacturing comprehensive upgrade sets for scale models since 2003 with the release of their first set for 1/35 scale armour. The company also produces turned aluminium barrels with muzzle brakes for both the late and early 8.8cm main guns of the Tiger in 1/35 scale and accessories in resin including Tiger I road wheels in transport mode. Shown below are 1. A generic 1/35 scale detail set for the mid production Tiger I. 2. Etched-brass details for the Trumpeter 1/35 scale early production Tiger I. 3. Metal Schürzen and fenders here applied to Dragon's 1/35 scale Tiger II.

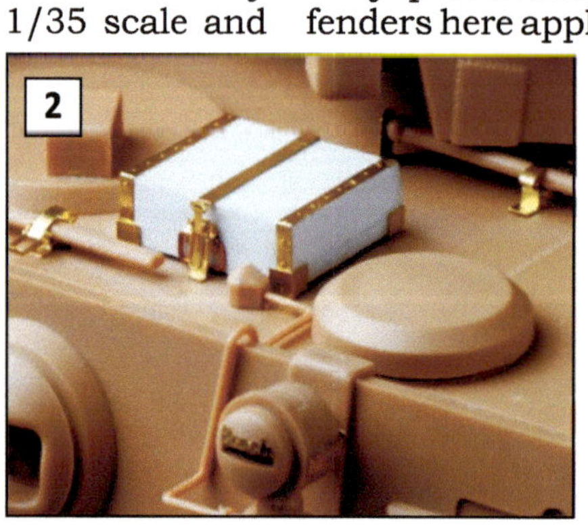

ABER

This Polish company has been manufacturing and selling upgrade sets since 1995 working in photo-etched brass, milled aluminium and brass, stainless steel and even wood. For some time now Tamiya has included Aber products with a number of their models. A full list of the accessories made specifically for the Tiger in all scales would be far toolarge to reproduce in this book and the reader can find the company's contact details on page 64. Shown here are, 1. Tiger II gun cleaning rods and their brackets in wood, brass and aluminium in 1/16 scale. 2. Photo-etched 1/35 scale details for the early production Tiger I. 3. Generic metal details for the Tiger II turret in 1/35 scale. 4, 5 and 6. 1/16 scale parts including a fire extinguisher, the early style muzzle brake as used on the Tiger I and Tiger II Porsche turrets and the Tiger I rear fender. 7. Details of the upgrade set for the Rye Field Models 1/35 scale early production Tiger I. 8. Barrel and muzzle brake in 1/35 scale for the 88 mm KwK 36 L/56 gun. 9. Details of the photo-etched brass set for the 1/35 scale late production Tiger I.

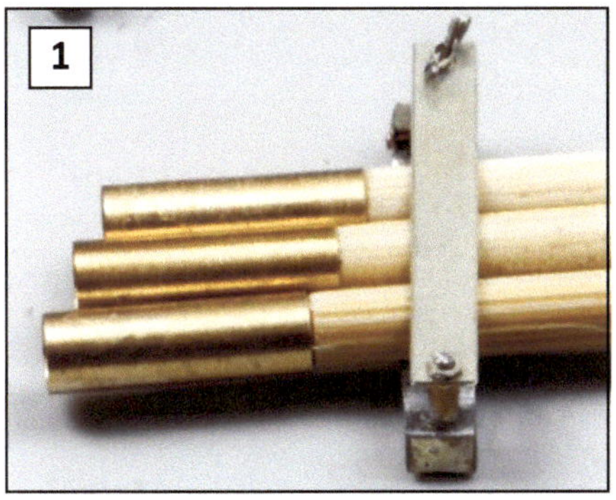
1

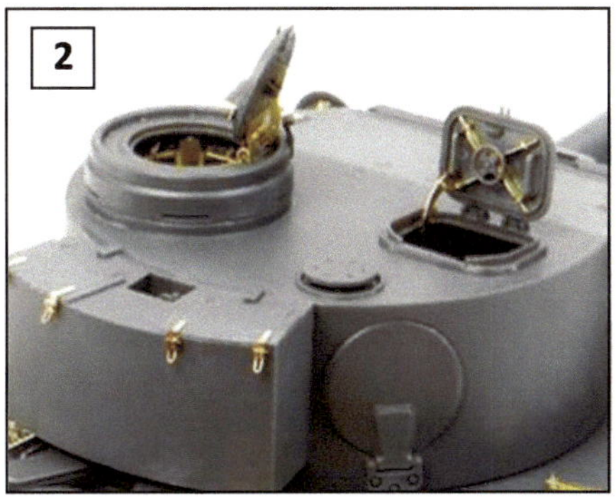
2

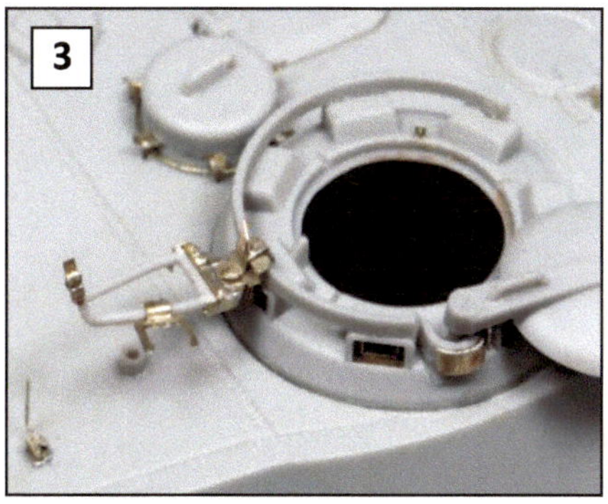
3

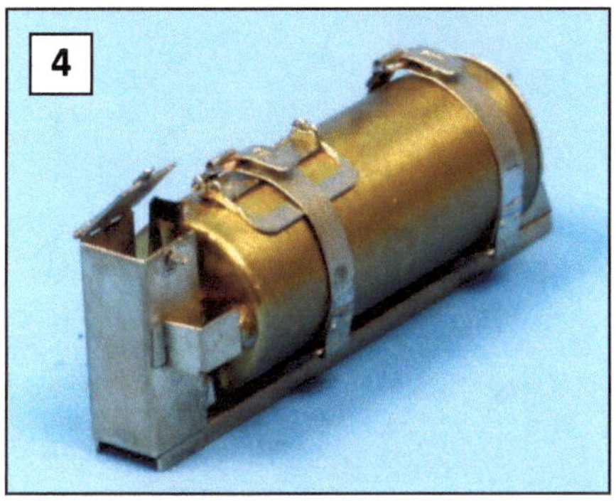
4

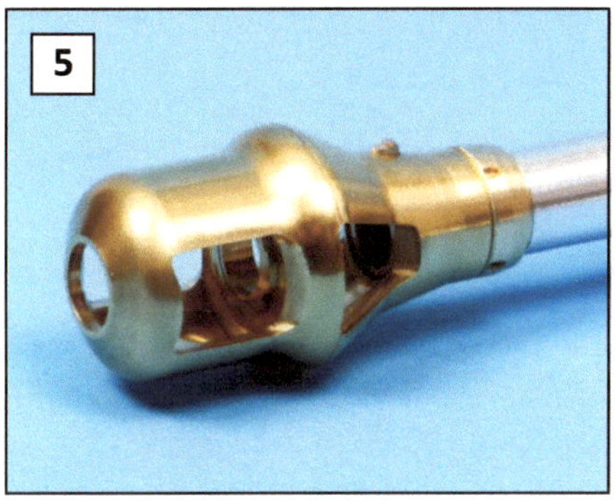
5

6

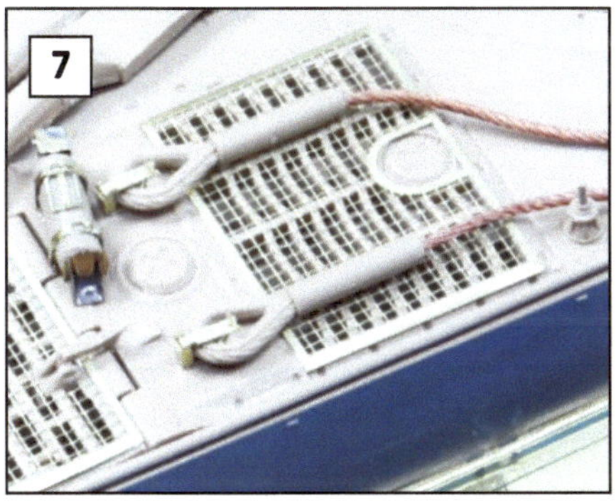
7

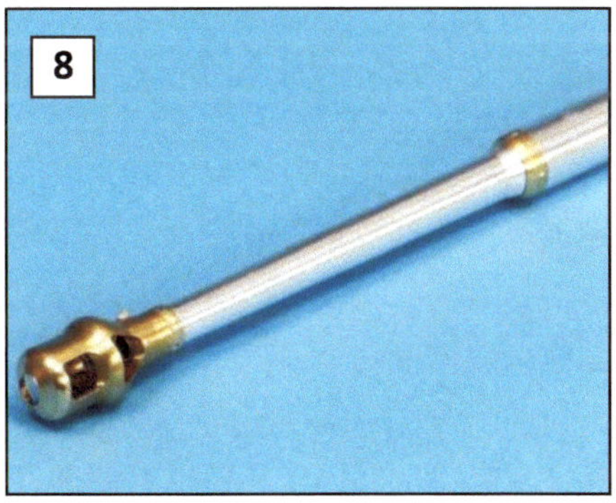
8

9

E.T. MODEL

This relatively new manufacturer from China, produces upgrade sets in 1/72 and 1/35 scale in brass and resin. Most sets are specifically designed, according to the company, to fit Dragon or Tamiya kits but some, for example the stowage bin, are referred to as universal. Shown below are the upgrade sets for, 1. Dragon Models' Tiger II. 2. Tamiya's 1/35 scale Tiger I mid production kit. 3. Meng-Model's Tiger II, also in 1/36 scale. The optional Zimmerit coating is included with the kit.

1

2

3

MODEL ARTISAN MORI

This small Japanese company produces resin upgrade parts for 1/35 scale armour models including detailed commander's cupolas for the Tiger I and Tiger II, for both the Porsche (1) and the Henschel (2) turrets, as well as more general items such as crew uniform (3) and tool sets, including fire extinguishers, tow shackles and bolt cutters, a 20 ton jack and Bosch headlights in kit form.

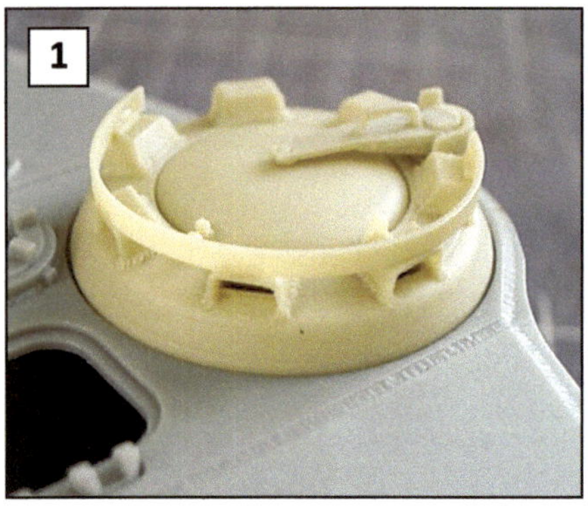

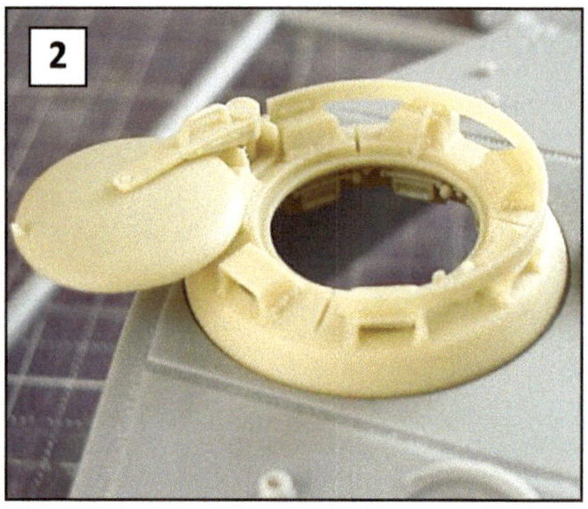

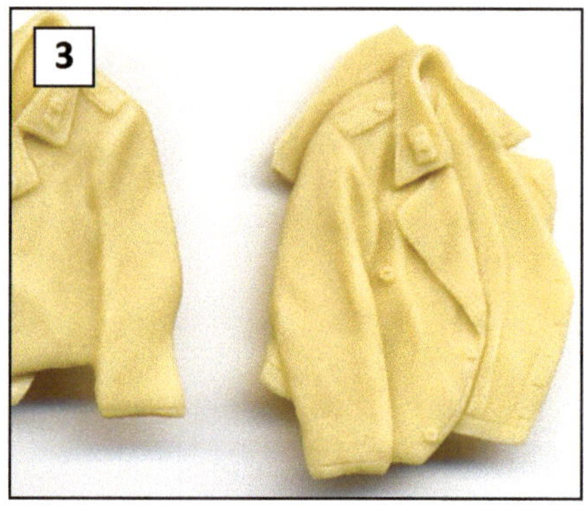

PANZER ART

Based in Poland this company produces a large range of resin parts for Second World War and modern era armoured vehicles in 1/35 scale. Shown here are, 1. A muzzle brake cover for the Tiger I. 2. Gun mantlet with casting marks for the Tiger II. 3. Strengthened gun mantlet for the Tiger I. 4. Spare road wheels. 5. Radio insulators and aerials. 6. Later wheels for the Tiger II.

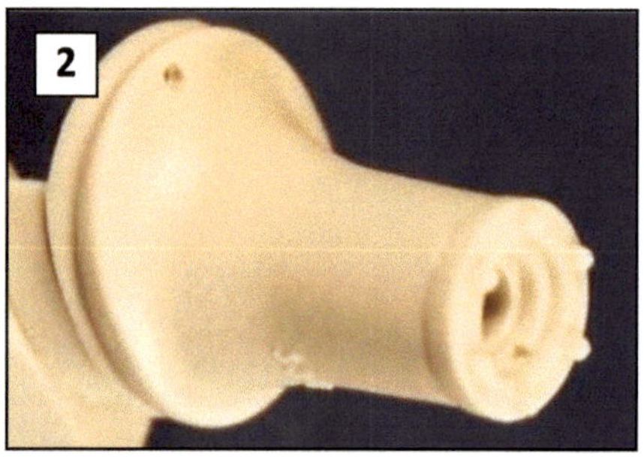

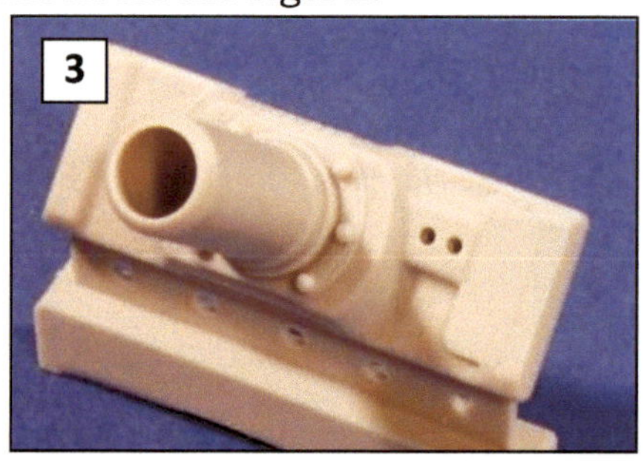

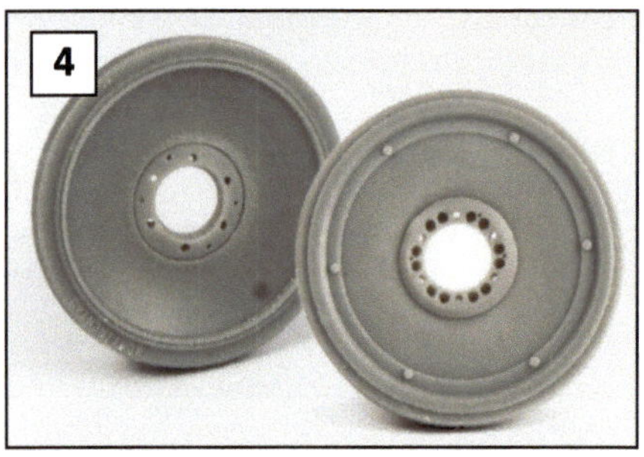

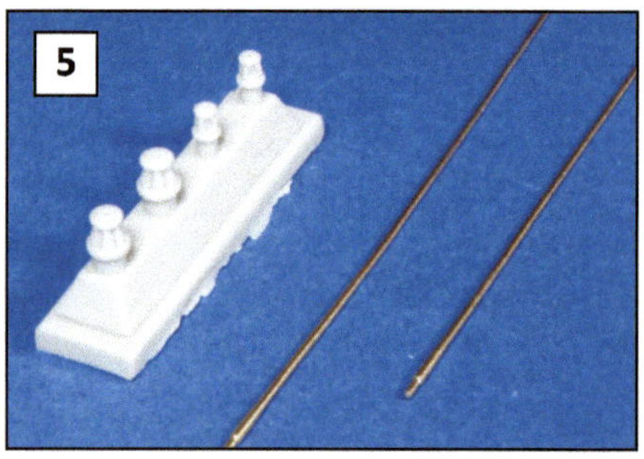

AFTERMARKET TRACKS

Most plastic kits today contain realistic tracks made from a form of vinyl which, unlike the older types, can be glued together, or hard plastic individual links. Nevertheless, there are many modellers who wish for the highest level of detail and realism possible and consequently the number of quality aftermarket products available seems to have increased in recent years, despite the extra expense and work required. Motorised models require workable tracks made up from individual links held together by pins, as were the full size items. The examples shown here, all in 1/35 scale, are 1. Later Tiger I tracks in white metal from Russian company Master Club. 2. Later Tiger I tracks in plastic from AFV Club. 3. Individual Tiger II track links in white metal from Spade Ace.

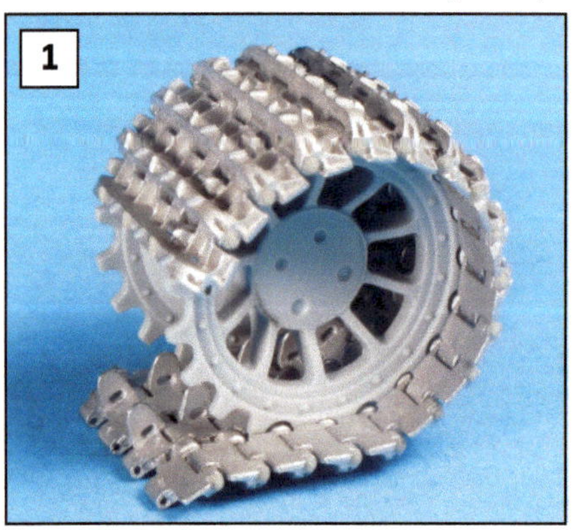

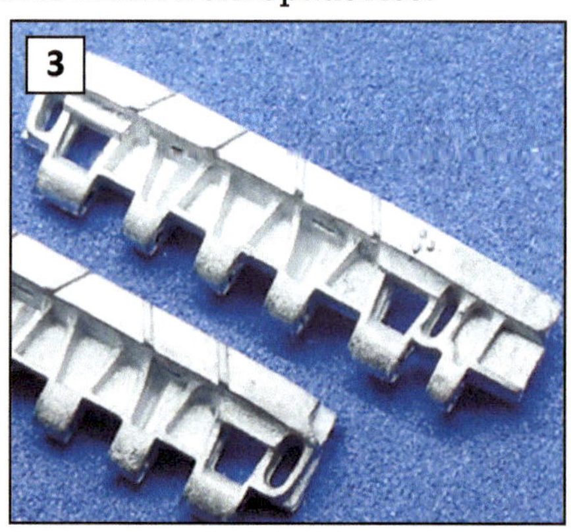

.........continued from page 15

Although it is not possible to list all the ad-hoc Kampfgruppen which took part in the battles of 1945 some mention should be made of units raised from the armour school and training facility at Bergen.

Kampfgruppe Grosan. Under the command of Oberst Erhard Grosan, who had had been the last commander of Panzertruppenschule Bergen, this formation contained a single Panther and two Tiger I tanks, two assault guns and a number of 7.5cm anti-tank guns. Much of the infantry element was made up from 2.Marine-Infanterie-Division.

The Kampfgruppe went into combat for the first time on 11 April 1945 near Engerhausen and although several of the anti-tank guns were lost, Grosan's men were able to hold up the British advance for two days. On 14 April one of the Tigers ran out of fuel and was left in Bassel, near Soltau, as a static defence position where, three days later, it was able to repel a British armoured reconnaissance unit. The remaining Tiger moved with the Panthers towards Bispingen, further to the east, where it too was able to hold up the British advance almost single-handedly until the following day when it was abandoned.

Tiger-Gruppe Fehrmann. During the first week of April 1945 the commander of the Lehrtruppe der Panzertruppenschule at Fallingbostel, Major Paul Schulze, was ordered to form a Kampfgruppe from whatever tanks he could obtain from the Bergen training facility. Major Schulze's unit had in fact been built from elements of the Panzer-Lehr-Division and had remained at Fallingbostel when the division left for the front in 1944 after completing its training.

The Kampfgruppe would eventually consist of five Panther and six Tiger I tanks, the latter commanded by Oberleutnant Rudolf Fehrmann, and a number of SdKfz 251 halftracks. The tanks of Tiger-Gruppe Fehrmann were marked on the turret side towards the front with a large letter F followed by a number. Sources differ on the numbers used but Wolfgang Schneider is adamant that they were 01, 02, 03, 04, 05 and 13. This is discussed further in the section on Hybrid Tiger assemblies on page 60.

Leaving Fallingbostel on 6 April 1945 and making their way to the front through the Schaumberger forest Major Schulze's Kampfgruppe went into action for the first time on 9 April 1945 at Wietersheim, about 40 kilometres east of Hanover, which was held by a force of British paratroopers (1).

In the brief fight that followed four of the Panthers were lost and one the Tigers damaged when a British PIAT anti-tank projectile struck the gun mantlet. Although most accounts state that this was Tiger F02, new research shows that it was almost certainly F01, probably the command tank of Oberleutnant Fehrmann, which was later photographed near Essel on the road to Ostenholz after it was disabled by a Comet of 3rd Royal Tank Regiment. The identification of this damaged Tiger as F01 at least explains why Fehrmann moved to another tank after the 9 April skirmish. Several photographs exist of Tiger F02 sitting on the crest of a small rise in an open field and the terrain is very similar to the area on the east side of the Aller near Rethem and it is possible that this was actually the tank abandoned on 6 April 1945. The Tiger with the damaged mantlet, under the command of Unteroffizier Franzen, returned to Fallingbostel on its own tracks and over the next few days was repaired.

Despite these setbacks Schulze's men were able to break through into the outskirts of Frille, north-east of Minden, and take prisoner thirty British soldiers who were holding the town.

On the following day, 10 April 1945, Schulze's remaining tanks pushed on to Bückeburg, a few kilometres to the south of Wietersheim, where two of his Tigers become bogged as they were negotiating a muddy track in a heavily wooded area. The surviving Panther attempted to recover the heavy tanks but also became bogged and as none of the tanks could be moved, Schulze ordered the crews to destroy all three (2). Shortly after this, Oberleutnant Fehrmann and the crews of the abandoned tanks, unable to keep up with Schulze, were captured by a unit of the US Army which had advanced from the south.

The remaining tanks moved on to Achum where they were engaged by an American armoured unit which was able to knock out Tiger F13, commanded Feldwebel Bellof, killing the entire crew. The last Tiger, number F05 with Major Schulze on board, accounted for three Sherman tanks and an armoured car before capturing a fuel truck complete with its cargo and maps.

During the night Major Schulze's Tiger, with the captured fuel truck, reached Lauenau and early the next morning passed through Nienstadt, directed by an American MP who failed to realize that they were Germans. On the western side of the town the Tiger ran into a column of Allied vehicles and after destroying a tank and an armoured car was also able to free about 200 German soldiers who had been held captive in a nearby barn. Now with a second American truck in tow, Major Schulze decided to head back towards the

Notes

1. What Schulze mistook for the front was actually some 30 kilometres behind the enemy lines. Not long after leaving Fallingbostel on 6 April, one of the Tigers broke down due to transmission failure and was abandoned near Rethem on the Aller River.

2. If the identification of the other Tigers given in this narrative is correct, the tanks abandoned in the forest near Bückeburg must have been F03 and F04, for which there are no known images.

Notes

1. These are the vehicles mention by Wolfgang Schneider. A report of 31 March 1945 prepared for the Inspector General of Armed Forces also includes at least three armed BIV ausf C Sprengstoffträger and a Steyr 8.8cm L/70 Waffenträger. The latter was thought to have only been built as a prototype and with the L/71 gun, but that may be a simple typo.

2. Throughout the war various stages of the call up were signalled by these codenames. Aktion Gneisenau announced the siphoning off of training establishment personnel to the field army.

German lines. On the same day, 12 April 1945, the Tiger of Unteroffizier Franzen, which had returned to Fallingbostel to be repaired, was ordered to move to Ostenholz and report to Kampfgruppe Grosan. Later that day Franzen's tank was involved in a firefight with three Comets of A Squadron, 3rd Royal tank Regiment and was able to destroy one before retiring.

At dawn on 13 April Major Schulze discovered a large Allied command post at Barsinghausen and made plans to attack it. However, the Tiger finally ran out of fuel at Hohenbostel, less than 2 kilometres short of their objective, and ordering the crew to destroy the tank, Major Schulze disbanded his Kampfgruppe. Later that morning, at about 10.30am, Unteroffizier Franzen's Tiger was knocked out by a British Comet tank.

Panzer-Kompanie Kummersdorf. Not to be confused with Panzer-Abteilung Kummersdorf which was absorbed by Panzer-Division Müncheberg and fought in Berlin, this formation was formed on 31 March 1945 and contained a Jagdtiger, four Panthers, two PzKpfw IV and a single PzKpfw III tank with one Hummel and one Nashorn self-propelled guns. In addition the company had a Tiger I and one Tiger II with the Porsche turret, although the latter could not be moved (1).

On 19 April 1945 the company was at Luchau, today a suburb of Hamburg, and may have seen some action here against the advancing British . On 21 April the company was ordered to join Kampfgruppe Möws which was at Zossen, south of Berlin.

Panzerkampfgruppe Nord. Raised by an order of 13 February 1945 as part of Aktion Gneisenau (2) this unit was to be made up of a headquarters with support platoons and a Panzergrenadier company all of which were taken from Panzertruppenschule Bergen.

The tank battalion was to be made up of a mixed company, including ten Panther and six Tiger tanks, and a light company both raised from the assets at Bergen.

A further mixed company with thirteen Panther and Tiger tanks and a light company were to be provided by Scheiss-Schule Putlos, the army's tank gunnery school. The formation was suspended by an order from Hitler on the advice of Generaloberst Guderian and later revived under Aktion Leuthen which came into effect on 24 March 1945.

Most of the units originally allocated to the Kampfgruppe were, however, used to form Panzer-Division Clausewitz or expended in small actions in the local area.

Tiger F01 of Tigergruppe-Fehrmann photographed some time after 13 April 1945 when it was knocked out by a British Comet tank. The location has been established as Hannoversche Strasse between Essel and Hademstorf just before the crossing of the Esseler Kanal. Maps from 1945 refer to the general area as the Esseler Wald and it is still heavily wooded today. The hole were the anti-tank round pierced the hull side is clearly visible as are the drum-style cupola and steel road wheels.

Panzergruppe Paderborn. Formed at the end of march 1945 as part of Aktion Leuthen this formation was raised from the assets of Panzer-Lehr-und Ausbildungs-Abteilung 'Tiger' based at Paderborn and was originally intended to reinforce Panzer-Ausbildungs-Verband Westfalen, an ad-hoc unit made up from reconnaissance and sniper training establishments.

Panzergruppe Paderborn was made up of eleven Tiger I and six Tiger II tanks and in addition to the personnel from Bergen, two of the Tiger I tanks were manned by surplus crews from 3.Kompanie, schwere Panzer-Abteilung 424 while three of the Tiger II tanks were operated by men from schwere Panzer-Abteilung 508, who had only recently returned from Italy (1).

During the last days of March the Tigers fought against the advancing US Army south of Paderborn with the crews of Panzer-Lehr-und Ausbildungs-Abteilung 'Tiger' who did not have tanks serving as infantry.

On 1 April the Tigers took part in an attack on Nordborchern and at nearby Bordchen a single tank was able to hold up the American advance. However, by the following day the tanks were running out of fuel and the Kampfgruppe commander, Hauptmann Uckert, was taken prisoner. Within 48 hours just one Tiger was able to move under its own power and the remains of Panzergruppe Paderborn reached the German lines at Veldrom, a small town south of Detmold.

On 12 April 1945 the new commander, Hauptmann Scharfe, reported that all the tanks had been lost or were inoperable, the latter presumably the lone Tiger that limped into Veldrom. A Tiger I tank of this formation is shown on page 19 of the Camouflage and Markings section.

Panzer-Lehr-Abteilung Putlos. This unit was formed in early April 1945, under the command of Major Walter von Bennigsen, from personnel of Scheiss-Schule Putlos and Panzer-Lehr-Abteilung Putlos, including the supply company.

On 16 April, as Kampfgruppe Bennigsen, it was absorbed by Panzer-Division Clausewitz.

Panzer-Division Clausewitz. Although this formation was in reality little more than a strong battle group it was officially the last Panzer division raised during the war.

Commanded by Generalleutnant Martin Unrein, a highly experienced and competent officer, the division was brought into being by an order of 4 April 1945 which stipulated that the organisation was to be completed and the division ready for operations within four days. But almost immediately it was learnt That the two most powerful components, Panzerjäger-Abteilung Grossdeutschland and parts of 325.Infanterie-Division, were so badly depleted by the fighting in the east that neither would be available for some weeks. In fact, The commander of 325.Infanterie-Division flatly refused to relinquish any part of his command. Although the Grossdeutschland battalion had lost all its recently issued Panzer IV/70(V) tank destroyers in the defence of East Prussia the crews eventually joined the division after being equipped with Sturmgeschütz III assault guns.

On 6 April, new orders were issued stating that Panzer-Division Clausewitz would be organised from remnants of various units made up from training establishments and elements of various understrength formations.

As can be imagined, at this stage of the war, this was not an orderly process and units were added to the division as they arrived and some never did, held up by transport problems or consumed by the Russian advance. In addition, battle casualties and constant re-organisations meant that the order of battle changed on an almost daily basis. Although strong in numbers of personnel the division lacked most of its authorised motor transport, particularly the Panzergrenadier companies which were in effect ordinary infantry units.

The division's armoured component consisted of the Panzerjäger battalion, a mixed or Gemischte Panzer regiment and a Panzer battalion formed from the tanks of Schiess-Schule Putlos, the German army's tank gunnery school. The latter contained two Tiger I tanks, one of which was disabled by a mine outside Fallersleben on 21 April 1945, while the other was eventually knocked out on the first day of May after holding up a British tank regiment for two days at Schwarzenbeck.

Elements of Panzer-Division Clausewitz first went into action on 12 April 1945, when a number of tanks and their supporting infantry stopped a strong British attack near the town of Uelzen, south of Lüneburg.

By the last days of April 1945, after almost continuous combat, the division had been reduced to a weak Kampfgruppe made up of an undersized infantry regiment and barely a company of tanks.

During its brief existence, three of the division's men, Major Gustav Walle, Leutnant Friedrich Anding and Obergefreiter Johann Stützle, all of Panzerjäger battalion, were either nominated for, or awarded, the Knight's Cross. The organisation, equipment and actions of this formation may be explored further in a future title.

Notes

1. Some sources give fifteen and three respectively. What is certain is that a total of eighteen Tiger I and nine Tiger II tanks were available at Paderborn at the time and I suspect that all nine of the latter were allocated to this Kampfgruppe but not combat-ready when it left for the front. Schneider states that fourteen tanks left Paderborn on 30 March 1945 while six remained behind in the repair facility.

Schwere SS-Panzer-Abteilung 501. After fighting in Normandy and during the retreat through France and Belgium this battalion was largely rebuilt and famously took part in the Ardennes Offensive which began on Saturday, 16 December 1944. The battalion's attacks against the town of Bastogne, and the corridor which had been formed in an effort to resupply the American troops surrounded there, continued into the new year with the last serious assault taking place on 3 January 1945.

Less than a week later, on 8 January, the battalion was withdrawn from the frontline, leaving two Tigers with the infantrymen of 340.Volksgrenadier-Division to act as a rearguard. However, by this time both the Americans and British were making advances in this area and the Tigers were forced to fight a series of running engagements from Lutremange and Malmedy to the area east of St.Vith. By 15 February 1945, when the tanks reached the relative safety of Blankenheim in Germany, the battalion's strength had been reduced to ten operational Tigers. From there they moved on to Brüggen and Brühl, south of Cologne, apparently on their own tracks, where they were loaded onto railcars and transported to Cottbus where the tanks were prepared for a move to Hungary.

The battalion's 1.Kompanie, which had been pulled out of the line on 30 December 1944, handed over their eight operational tanks to the second and third companies and what are possibly two of these vehicles are shown and discussed on page 17 of the Camouflage and Markings section. On 6 January 1945 the first company, which had been waiting in the town of Oerlinghausen, south-east of Bielefeld, was ordered to pick up six new tanks from Truppenübungsplatz Senne while the remaining crews moved a short distance to Schloss Holte-Stukenbrock on the western edge of the Sennelager training grounds The six Tigers and their crews were ordered to the east and reached Breslau on 19 January, continuing on to Hungary in the first days of February 1945. At the same time the men at Schloss Holte-Stukenbrock, who had been joined by a number of fresh recruits, began training on a single Tiger II which had been with the battalion since the battles of September 1944.

By the end of February 1945 the company had been issued thirteen Tigers and on 3 March they were sent to the east first to Dresden and then, for some unknown reason, ordered back to Sennelager. A number of the company's officers, including Hauptsturmführer Dr. Wolfgang Rabe, the battalion surgeon who had been acting as the company commander, continued on to Hungary. On 12 March the company's tanks were handed over to schwere Panzer-Abteilung 506 and the crews returned to Oerlinghausen to resume training on the veteran Tiger II which had apparently been left there. On 1 April 1945, learning that the Americans were nearby, the Tiger was made operational and, commanded by Untersturmführer Rolf Henniges, moved off towards the north in the

Photographed in Hungary, possibly during the summer of 1945, this Tiger II of schwere Panzer-Abteilung 501 is one of the thirty-two tanks the battalion lost between February and May 1945. In another image of this vehicle the company number 332 is visible on the turret side and looks to have been painted over here. As that number was allocated to one of the vehicles destroyed in the Ardennes this Tiger may be one of the 1.Kompanie tanks that survived the battles there or one of the six replacements received on 26 January 1945.

A Tiger II of schwere SS-Panzer-Abteilung 502 photographed near Küstrin in eastern Germany in April or May 1945. This formation received no replacements after leaving Sennelager in the first half of March and this tank provides a good illustration of the appearance of the battalion's Tigers during early 1945. Note that an area of the turret side has been roughly painted over to accommodate the Balkenkreuz.

direction of Senne. Reaching a railway station the tank was hit by a Panzerfaust, mistakenly fired by a German soldier, which killed Henniges and three of his crew (X). Later that day Unterstürmfuhrer Heinz Buchner and a new crew managed to get the Tiger moving again and headed off towards the American positions along what is today Bundesautobahn 2. The tank reached a location given as '500 metres east of the Elbrechter farmhouse' when it was hit by an anti-tank round and began to burn (X).

With the Allies so close Schloss Holte-Stukenbrock was evacuated and the tank crews fought their way through to Seesen in the Harz Mountains and from there some managed to rejoin the other companies of the battalion which had retreated through Austria to Steyr.

Schwere SS-Panzer-Abteilung 502. This battalion fought in the Normandy campaign and the retreat through France, losing its last Tiger near Genval in Belgium, less than 5 kilometres from the Waterloo battlefield, on 1 September 1944 when it was destroyed by its own crew.

The battalion was rebuilt over the following months, receiving six new Tiger II tanks on 27 December. These were later handed over to schwere SS-Panzer-Abteilung 503 which was being formed at the time, and it was not until 6 March 1945 that the battalion received the last of thirty-one tanks. This was still fourteen tanks short of the authorised allocation but the battalion was nevertheless ordered to be ready for an immediate move to the east. As the tanks were preparing to move the commander of the second company, Obersturmführer Soretz, was killed in a car accident becoming the battalion's last casualty of many in the west. After a lengthy journey by rail the battalion arrived on the Eastern Front during the evening of 19 March 1945 and within days the Tigers were fighting around Küstrin.

SS-Brigade Westfalen. This unit is sometimes referred to as SS-Ersatz-Brigade Westfalen and SS-Panzer-Brigade Westfalen and was purely an ad-hoc formation. I have included it here to avoid confusion with the similarly named Panzer-Ausbildungs-Verband Westfalen (see Panzergruppe Paderborn).

Commanded by Obersturmbannführer Hans Stern the brigade was made up of two weak infantry regiments bolstered by the Tiger II tanks and Jagdpanther tank destroyers of schwere Panzer-Abteilung 507 and later by three Jagdtigers from schwere Panzerjäger-Abteilung 512. Claims that Stern's formation could field sixty Tiger and Panther tanks are completely groundless.

In March 1945 SS-Brigade Westfalen was committed to the fighting in an attempt to prevent the encirclement of Heeresgruppe B in the Ruhr Pocket and although interesting, the story of this Kampfgruppe is beyond the remit of this book.

Notes

1. Schneider gives the location as Kraks which no longer seems to exist. It may have been along the current Krakser Strasse which runs parallel to the road to Senne from Schloss Holte. The soldier who fired the Panzerfaust immediately deserted but was found and executed several days later.
2. The Elbrechter farmhouse is not shown on any modern map but could not have been any further west than the village of Hasselbachaue which, according to the US 12th Army Group situation map for 1 April 1945, was in American hands on that day.

SCHWERE SS PANZER-ABTEILUNG 501, LATE 1944-EARLY 1945

The battalion was rebuilt with forty-five Tiger II tanks prior to the Ardennes Offensive and remained in the west until 16 January 1945. The vehicles shown here in a lighter shade are those known to have been destroyed between 18 December 1944 and 8 January 1945 in the battles in Belgium. Of the remaining tanks just eighteen were fully operational. A unique aspect of this battalion was the fourth company made up of the support elements that were officially attached to the battalion headquarters. The Sdkfz 251/9 halftracks reported on hand on 30 December 1944 were almost certainly allocated to this company. Another report, dated 15 January 1945, the day before the battalion left for the Eastern Front, stated that two of the four original Bergepanthers allocated to the Werkstatt-Kompanie were still serviceable.

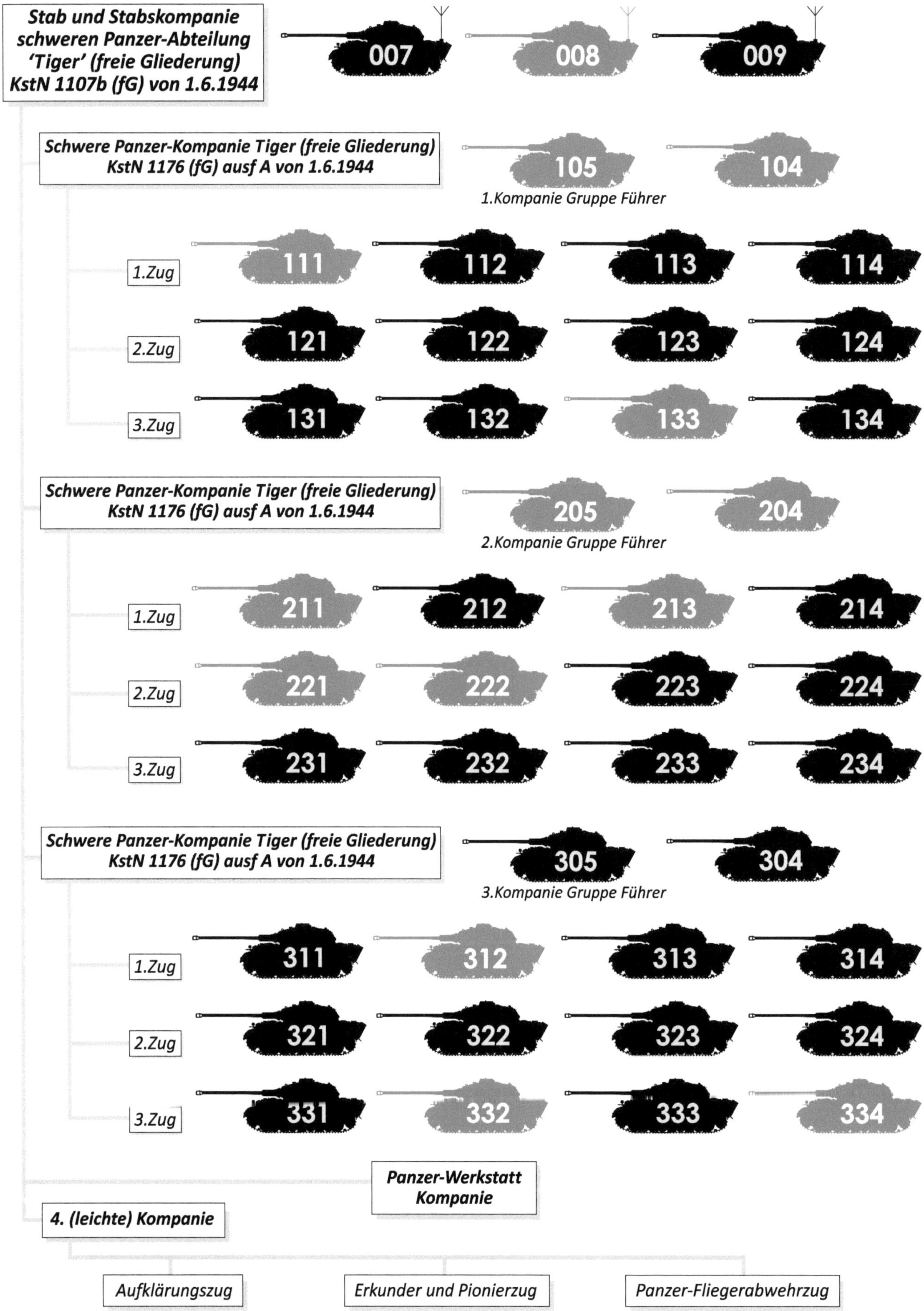

Between late 1942, when the first Tiger I tanks were issued to operational units, and March 1945, when the last Tiger II rolled off the assembly line at Kassel, the design of both these heavy armoured vehicles was subject to almost constant change and upgrading. The modifications applied to the Tiger I during production were covered in some detail in the first book in this series, Tiger I and Tiger II Tanks: German Army and Waffen-SS Eastern Front 1944 and the tenth title, Tiger I: German Army Heavy Tank, Southern Front North Africa, Sicily and Italy 1942-1945, and for that reason I have chosen to concentrate here on the Tiger II. In fact a relatively small number of Tiger I tanks took part in the battles of winter 1944 and spring 1945, with just thirty-one of these vehicles recorded as being available to Oberbefehlshaber West on the eve of the Ardennes Offensive. A number of older production models, which had been used by training establishments, were pressed into service but these were few in number and many are covered in the Camouflage and Markings section. The hybrid versions of the Tiger I, which appeared late in the war, are examined separately on page 60.

The Tiger II was not a development of the Tiger I but rather a completely new design intended from the first as a replacement for the first heavy tank. As a general economy measure, it was envisaged that the Tiger II and the proposed Panther II would eventually share a number of important features, particularly the steering gear and tracks, and the basic silhouette of the Tiger II owes more to the Panther than it did to its predecessor.

The firms of Porsche GmbH and Henschel und Sohn were invited to compete for the design of the hull and suspension and the latter's submission was finally accepted for production. During the development stage, Friedrich Krupp AG had been contracted to build the turrets for both the Porsche and Henschel hulls and had partly completed 100 units before 17 February 1943 when the order was cancelled. Even at that early stage concerns had been raised over the possibility of the curved turret front acting as a shot trap, deflecting anti-tank rounds downwards through the roof of the hull. Although this is the reason most often given, the turret's complexity of construction and the inadequacy of the frontal armour were also important factors. Krupp's engineers began work Immediately on a new turret and although the final product was superficially similar to the original offering it was in fact an almost complete re-design.

It was decided, however, that since fifty of the original turrets could be made ready in a very short time, they were to be utilised as an interim measure and all were handed over to Wegmann & Co., located in Kassel close to the Henschel plant, where they were fitted with a number of standard components such as hydraulic drives as the Porsche proposal for the hull employed an electric drive. Before leaving the Krupp plant the original 25mm thick roof plates of each turret were cut out and replaced with plates of 40mm thickness. As many as sixteen of these turrets, perhaps more, had a hole cut in the turret side on the left for the commander's viewing port or Schaulock which was plugged and welded shut. On tanks coated with Zimmerit, as most of these vehicles were, this appears as a flat circular area in the turret's curved side. These turrets were fitted to the first Henschel production hulls, beginning with Fahrgestellnummer, or chassis number, 280001 although the sequence was interrupted after 280047. The new Krupp turret was accepted for

This early turret was taken from a captured tank and stripped of its Zimmerit coating and paint. The curve of the left side is apparent here and the weld beads highlight the complex construction of this component. This is one of the turrets built without the Schaulock and the pistol port has been plugged and welded shut.

production as the Serien-Turm or series turret, sometimes called the Produktions Turm, and was fitted to the production hulls starting with Fahrgestellnummer 280048.

Today the original fifty turrets are often erroneously referred to as the Porsche Turm, while the production turret is just as incorrectly known as the Henschel Turm. Both turrets were designed and largely constructed by Krupp with the final assembly completed by Wegmann. A number of lesser concerns such as Leitz, Wetzlar, Mitteldeutsche Stahlwerke and Sonderring Walzlager contributed smaller parts including the optics for the main gun and the turret trace and traversing mechanism. Once the construction of the turret was complete the final assembly was undertaken at Henschel's Kassel plant, just a short distance from the Wegmann factory. Each chassis was given its own unique number or Fahrgestellnummer (Fgst) while each turret could also be identified by a number, here referred to as a Turm Nr. As with the Tiger I a number of modifications were carried out before production ceased in March 1945 and the most important are listed below. Although the terms Porsche and Henschel turret are indeed incorrect they are in such widespread use today, particularly among model manufacturers, that I have continued to use these names here and throughout this book as a matter of convenience. Similarly, the Tiger II is more correctly referred to as Pzkw VI Tiger ausf B but I have used both names here.

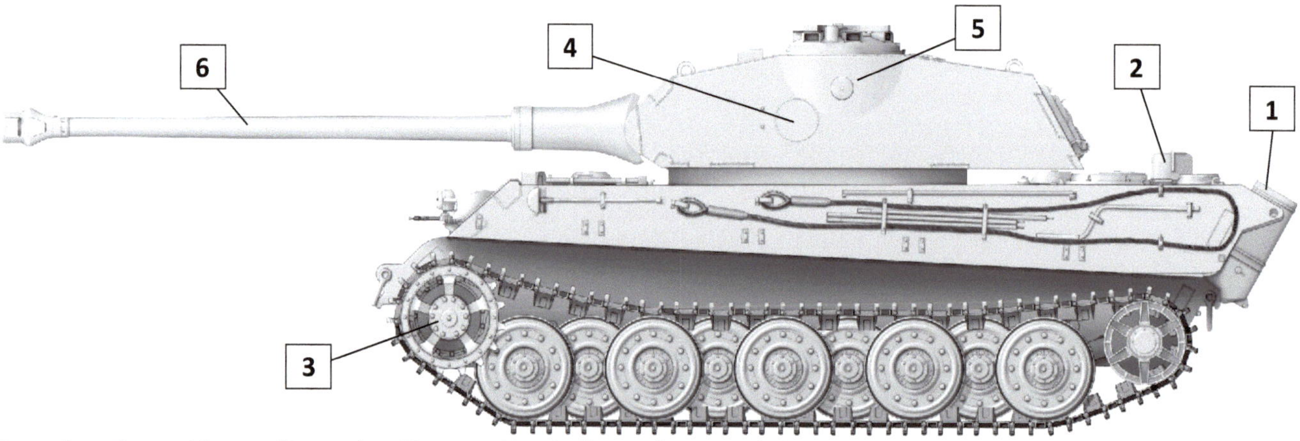

Panzerkampfwagen Tiger ausf B, completed January 1944. The first production tanks had the standard tool stowage, sheet metal covers (1) for the exhausts and 40mm armour plate added to the turret roof as described in the text. The prominent armoured cover (2) over the opening for the deep-wading equipment on the rear deck was fitted to the first production models but very quickly dropped. Note the early 18-tooth drive sprocket (3) and the lack of a turret guard ring. The view port, or Schauloch, on the turret side (4) next to the pistol port (5), was welded shut as shown here. The single piece mono-bloc gun barrel (6) was replaced in production during April 1944. The curved track guards, hull Schürzen an coating of Zimmerit, which these tanks certainly had, have been omitted for clarity.

January 1944. From Fgst Nr.280001, the first production Tiger II, the flat front fenders of the prototype were replaced by a curved version with fixed sideplates (A). A coat of Zimmerit anti-magnetic mine paste, which had been introduced into tank manufacture the previous September, was applied from the start of production.

February 1944. The first pattern, upright exhaust pipes were replaced by curved models (B) and the metal shields for the exhausts were dropped from production. An access port with an armoured cover for the blowtorch, used to heat the engine's cooling water in cold weather, was added on the rear plate below the left exhaust.

April 1944. A notch was cut from the edge of the glacis in front of the radio operator's periscope (C) to allow a better field of view. The hull front extensions were modified to allow for the carrying of C hooks and the hull extensions at the rear were modified to allow the hooks to pivot upwards. A turret ring guard was added to the hull for tanks with the Porsche turret. The T.Z.F 9b/1 binocular gunsight (D) was replaced by the T.Z.F.9d monocular model. With this change a single aperture for the gunsight was adopted and the redundant apertures were plugged and welded shut. This feature is almost impossible to discern on tanks coated with Zimmerit. A new two-piece gun tube was introduced to

replace the original monobloc version of the Kwk 43 L/71 gun. A lighter muzzle brake was also introduced.

May 1944. A new double link track, designated Gelandekette Gg 26/800/300 replaced the Gg 24/800/300 design which had been fitted to the first production vehicles. These new tracks Were also retrofitted to older tanks. The drive sprocket (A) for the new tracks had nine teeth in place of the previous eighteen. A metal blade sight (B) for the commander was mounted on the turret roof at the left front corner. This was lined up with two wires welded over the foremost periscope of the commander's

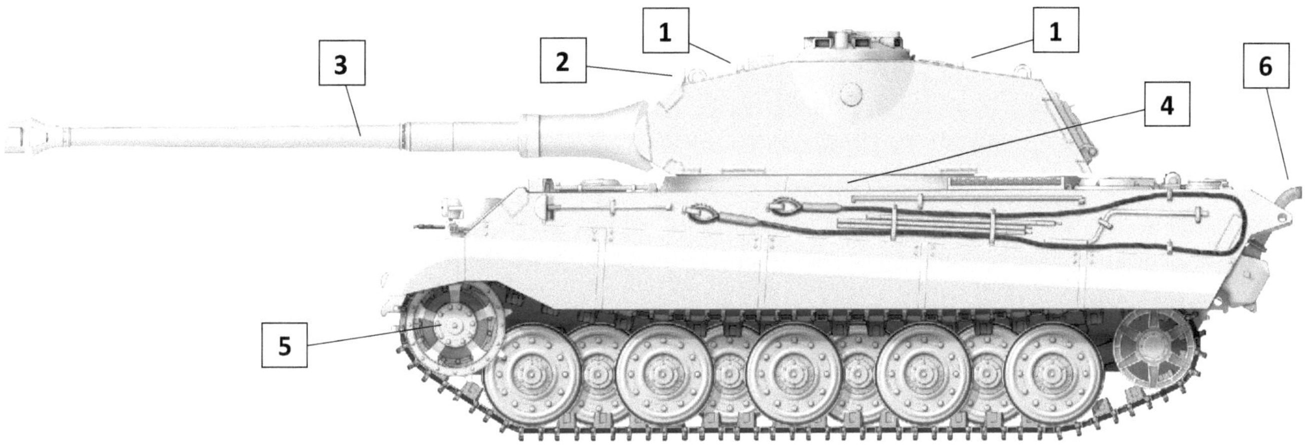

Panzerkampfwagen Tiger ausf B, completed June 1944. This tank has the sockets (1), or Pilzen, welded to the turret roof, the commander's blade sight in front of the forward lifting eye (2), the two-piece gun tube (3), the turret ring guard (4), the nine-tooth drive sprocket introduced with the Gg 26/800/300 tracks (5) and the curved exhaust pipes (6). The armoured cover for the deep-wading equipment and the metal guards for the engine exhausts have been dropped form production. Not visible in our drawing is the notch in the glacis in front of the driver's periscope, the single aperture for the monocular gun sight and the vent on the rear deck for the fuel system. This tank would also have been coated in Zimmerit.

June 1944. The armoured pot-shaped cover (D) for the deep wading equipment was deleted and replaced by a heavy wire mesh screen. This modification had in fact been carried out on most production Tigers but became standard in June. Three sockets or Pilzen (C) were welded to the turret roof to hold the 2ton jib boom and these were also retrofitted to older models. A new, 40 mm thick loader's hatch (E) was introduced. From Fgst Nr.280048 the Serien-Turm or series turret with strengthened, sloping front plate and without the bulge under the cupola was introduced and the turret ring guard, which was no longer necessary, was dropped from production.

July 1944. Hangers and fasteners (F) were welded to both sides of the turret to hold double lengths of spare track. Small brackets (G) for poison gas identification panels were welded to the top of the gun mantlet and the turret roof at the right rear corner. Units in the field were ordered to replace the 18-tooth drive sprocket ring with the new 9-tooth version. This was sometimes accomplished by cutting out every second tooth.

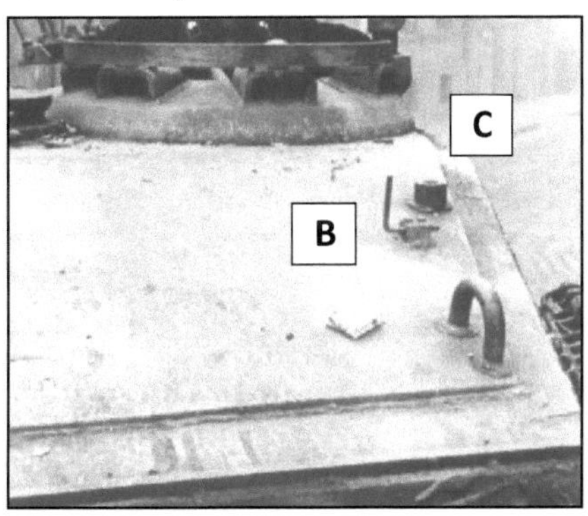

August 1944. Between April and August three additional Krupp designed turrets were completed and fitted to Henschel chassis, making a total of fifty. Narrower tracks (A), Verladekette, were provided for railway transport. To distinguish these tracks from those used for the Tiger I (B), two or three links out of every ten were supposed to have been painted red. A redesigned commander's cupola (D) was introduced, mounted in a machined recess and secured by seven bolts. On 19 August 1944 an army order was issued directing that tanks were now to be painted in a standardised colour scheme before leaving the assembly plant. The factory-applied camouflage schemes are examined in detail on page 62. From Fgst Nr.280177, the interiors were no longer painted in Elfenbein RAL 1001, a very light, ivory shade, but left in their coat of RAL 8012, a red oxide primer.

September 1944. An order of 9 September directed that the application of Zimmerit (C) was to cease immediately. It was widely believed among tank crews that small arms fire could ignite the anti-magnetic mine paste possibly causing a fire. Although the army high command was able to easily disprove this, it was probably seized upon as a convenient excuse to discontinue what had been a costly and largely useless practice (1). The armour manufacturers were ordered to weld an inverted u-shaped guard over the gunsight aperture (E). As a large number of turrets had already been delivered to the assembly plants this feature is not commonly seen before January 1945.

October 1944. From Fgst Nr.280255 a circular plate was bolted over the opening for the deep wading gear on the rear deck. This modification was also to be retrofitted by units in the field. As the jack (F) was no longer issued with the Tiger II the brackets on the rear hull plate were dropped from production. Units in the field were ordered to discontinue the application of Zimmerit. An order of 31 October stipulated that Henschel was to

Notes

1. Neither the Russians nor the western allies employed magnetic mines of their own design during the Second World War which meant that, in the great majority of cases, the application of Zimmerit was totally unnecessary. Indeed, US Army intelligence officers firmly believed, until the end of the war, that Zimmerit was a form of camouflage.

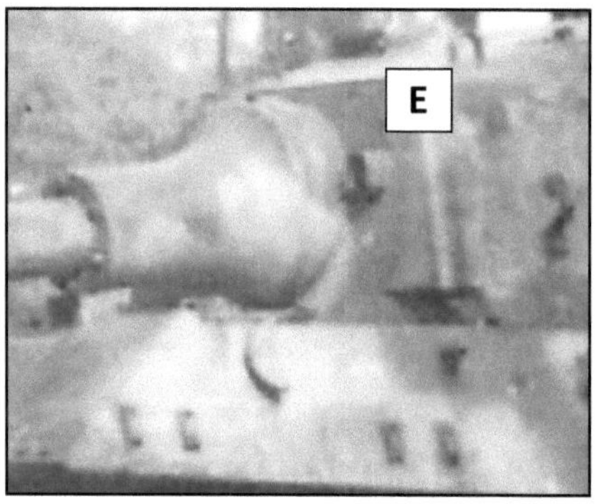

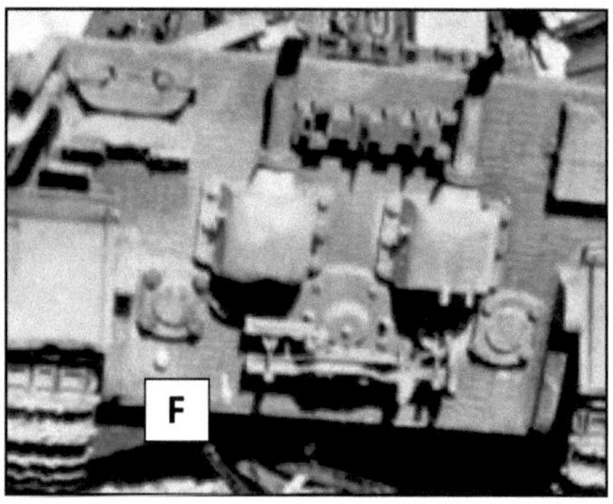

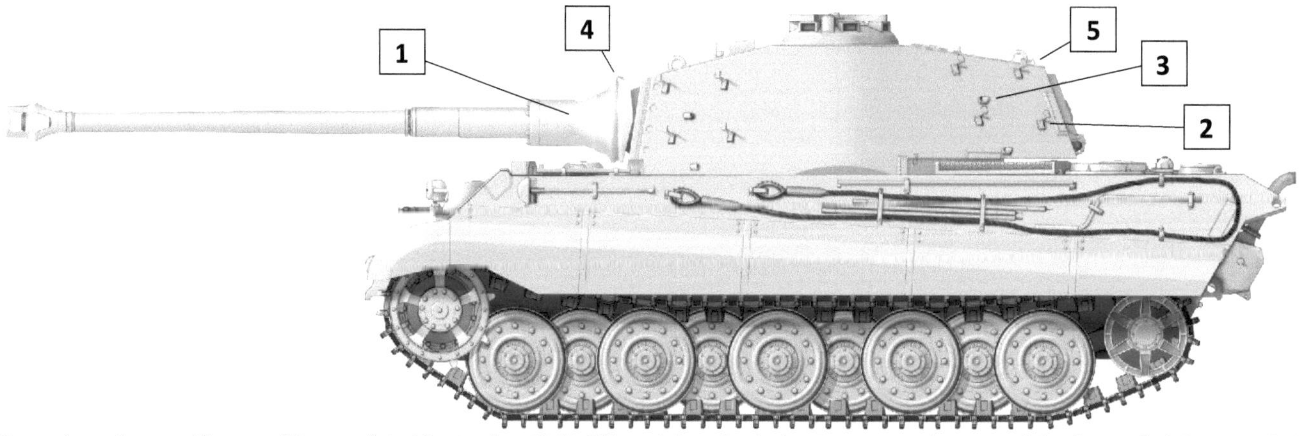

Panzerkampfwagen Tiger ausf B, completed September 1944. This tank has the Serien-Turm or series turret (1), often called the Henschel turret, introduced in June 1944 with the later gun mantlet and with hangers (2) and fasteners (3) for spare track links. Small brackets for poison gas detection panels are fixed to the top of the gun mantlet (4) and behind the lifting eye on the turret roof at the rear (5). Not visible in our drawing are the armoured guards for the torsion bars on turret rear, the armoured cover over the engine compartment on the rear deck and the 40mm thick loader's hatch introduced in June 1944.

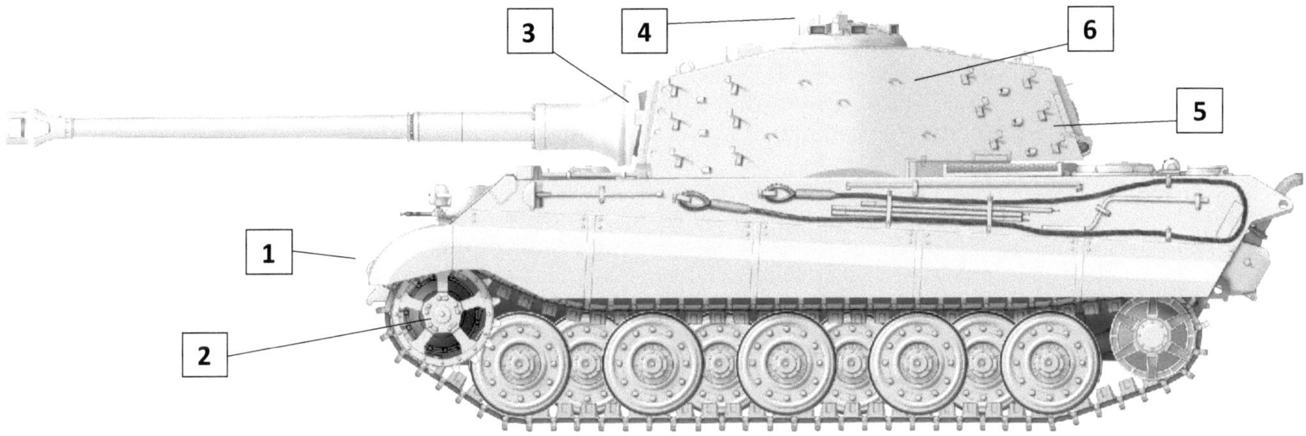

Panzerkampfwagen Tiger ausf B, completed March 1945. This tank has the reinforced front track guards (1), the single link Kgs 73/800/15 tracks and 18-tooth drive sprocket (2). The turret has the metal rain guard over the sight aperture (3) and the post mount (4) for the anti-aircraft machine gun which replaced the ring of the commander's cupola. Also visible are the spare track hangers and fasteners for the single link tracks (5) and five loops (6) to hold foliage camouflage.

cease the use of Dunkelgelb RAL 7028 as a base colour for armoured vehicles and introduced a new system which is further discussed on page 62.

November 1944. Units in the field were ordered to weld track hangers, Erasatzkettenglieder, to the turret sides, a feature which had been incorporated into production in the previous July.

December 1944. An order of 20 December introduced a completely revised camouflage scheme that was to be applied before the tanks left the assembly plant. This is discussed in detail on page 62.

January 1945. As an experiment, approval was given to fit armour plates over the air intakes on the rear deck of Tiger II Fgst Nr.280404 as a defence against fire from enemy aircraft. It is unlikely that this innovation was ever introduced into production.

March 1945. New curved track guards (A and B), reinforced with raised vertical ribs were incorporated into production. Single link Kgs 73/800/152 tracks, sometimes referred to as cross-country tracks (C and D), were introduced and three sets of track hangers were to be welded onto the turret sides (F). The single link tracks also saw the reintroduction of an 18-tooth drive sprocket (E). The metal ring for the anti-aircraft machine gun welded to the tops of the periscopes of the commander's cupola was dropped from production and replaced by a simple post fixed to the left front periscope. Five semi-circular loops were welded to each side of the turret to hold foliage camouflage (G). The brackets which held the wooden jack block and the fasteners for the track mounting cable were both dropped from production.

As no more than thirty completed vehicles were accepted by the Waffenamt during March, very few of the modifications introduced in that month are seen on tanks in the field.

One technical aspect which was not covered in the earlier titles in this series are the so-called Hybrid vehicles based on the Tiger I which typically incorporate features of early and late production models. Exactly why these tanks were assembled in such a way is not fully understood and much of our knowledge comes from photographic evidence.

They cannot be accounted for among the last fifty-four Tigers assembled by Henschel between the last week of June and the middle of August 1944. These tanks, numbered in the Fgst.Nr. 251293 to 251346 series, were built from recycled hulls and thirty-two recycled turrets. The remaining twenty-two turrets were new, assembled from replacement parts. The order for these tanks stipulated that they be upgraded to the latest production standards which specifically mentioned the installation of a cast commander's cupola and new loader's hatch. Importantly, any turrets with the 25mm thick turret roof, replaced in production from March 1944, were to receive new 40mm plates. This meant that the older drum-style cupola could no longer be fitted. No mention is made of the wheels and small production modifications such as the notch cut into the hull extensions may have been ignored but these tanks, in theory at least, would have been similar to any mid or late production version. In his exhaustive, two-volume account of the Tiger battalions Oberst Wolfgang Schnieder mentions that Panzer-Kompanie Hummel, a unit which served exclusively in the west, was formed in July 1944 with fourteen Tiger I tanks, a number of which were obtained from maintenance facilities and that some of these had features of both early and late model production vehicles. Indeed, a photograph of one of the company's tanks disabled during the fighting in the Ardennes near Oberwampach, clearly shows an early production turret fitted to what appears to be a mid-production hull with later rubber-cushioned, steel-tired road wheels. Another photograph of what is almost certainly one of this company's Tigers, also taken in the Ardennes area, may have an early turret but it is obscured by foliage camouflage making and definitive identification impossible. However, there is no real evidence that the Tiger I of this company, numbered 111, that was disabled and abandoned in April 1945 near Brunskappel, is a Hybrid and it was most likely an early production tank. This vehicle is shown in the Camouflage

At right: The Hybrid Tiger I of Panzer-Kompanie Hummel. This tank was disabled while the company was attached to schwere Panzer-Abteilung 506 as the battalion's fourth company during the fighting in the Ardennes. Below; The tanks of Tigergruppe Fehrmann mentioned in the text.

Said to be from schwere Panzer-Abteilung 424, this Hybrid Tiger I was photographed in the Polish town of Czestochowa in January 1945. Although equipped with Tiger II tanks at this time, the battalion was able to absorb assets from other units, in particular the last Tiger I tanks of schwere Panzer-Abteilung 509, and reported that a total of fifty-three tanks were on hand at the beginning of October. This photograph shows that these types of tanks could be encountered on both fronts and that workshops were capable of assembling them. Note the Pzkpfw IV stowage bin on the turret rear.

and Markings section on page 18. Also operating on the Western Front at this time, schwere Panzer-Abteilung 301 (Fkl) may have had at least one Hybrid Tiger I on hand which was eventually captured in Cologne in early 1945 and also photographed extensively at Sennelager after the war. This tank is shown on page 19 of the Camouflage and Markings section of this book.

The most famous Hybrid Tigers are probably those fielded by Tigergruppe Fehrmann in April 1945 but even these may not have been as numerous as is often supposed. Under the command of Oberleutnant Rudolf Fehrmann this unit, as part of Kampfgruppe Schulze, contained six Tiger I tanks. Schneider's account states that these tanks were number as F01, F02, F03, F04, F05 and F13 with the first letter standing for the commander's name (1). In any case, I have only been able to locate definitive photographic evidence for tanks F01, F02, F13 and a very poor quality image of what is probably F05. Of those F01 is certainly a Hybrid model built with an early turret and a mid-production hull fitted with steel road wheels. The turret and hull were both coated with Zimmerit past at one time which has been damaged by enemy fire. The turret has a set of track hangers on the left hand side but none on the right and it is possible to see where the smoke candle dischargers were removed. A number of clear photographs shown that F02 is an early production tank fitted with rubber-rimmed road wheels. Here too, it is possible to see evidence of the smoke candle dischargers confirming that these turrets were originally assembled before June 1943. Almost certainly, it was at one time completely coated with Zimmerit which has been removed or worn off the turret before the number was applied. Another noticeable feature is the lack of a rear stowage bin.

The available photographs of F13 all seem to have been taken after most of the road wheels had been removed but the last wheel, next to the rear idler on the left hand side, does appear to be one of the steel-tired models confirming that this tank was indeed a Hybrid. Interestingly, Fred Hawkins, a veteran of the RAF who actually took a number of these photographs was adamant that F13 was predominantly dark grey with a distinctive hand-painted turret number rendered in red with a white outline. The images of Tiger F05, which was commanded by Major Schulze at one time, are too indistinct to comment with any certainty about the technical details.

What can be said with some confidence, however, is that the Tigers of Kampfgruppe Schulze had all been instruction vehicles based at the huge Fallingbostel training area and were probably considered adequate for that task. They were only thrown into combat as an extreme emergency measure and it is entirely possible that they had been cobbled together from different vehicles by the training facilities own workshops.

Notes

1. This has been challenged in recent times but it should be remembered that Oberst Schneider had access to official documents and many German language accounts and often qualifies his work if there is some doubt.

The first Tiger I tanks to enter service in late 1942 were painted in a base coat of RAL 7021 Dunkelgrau or in one of the newly introduced tropical colours in the case of the companies sent to Tunisia.

On 18 February 1943 an order issued by the Oberkommando des Heeres (OKH) introduced a system where armoured vehicles were painted in a new colour referred to at the time as Dunkelgelb nach Muster, or dark yellow (1). Formations in the field were be provided with two camouflage colours, initially RLM Olivgrün and Rotbraun RAL 8017, in the form of a paste in either 2 or 20 kilogram tins which could be diluted with either water or petrol, the latter apparently giving the best result.

The February order also saw the end to the practice of units sourcing paint directly from the suppliers and, importantly, the April directive contained a table indicating the exact amount of paint required, by weight, to paint certain types and classes of vehicle. Once diluted the paint could be applied by brush or spray gun and although the essence of the new system was that the style of camouflage was left to the initiative of local commanders, the need for economy was strongly implied. This order covered all units of the army including those operating in northern Europe, the Mediterranean and the Soviet Union and there is some evidence that it was in part an effort to standardise a practice where unauthorised colours were being used. The 1943 system would remain in force until mid-August 1944 and as production of the Tiger I had all but ceased by that time most of those tanks would have been delivered in the RAL 7028 base coat.

On 19 August 1944 the Heereswaffenamt (2) advised the assembly plants that the practice of units in the field creating their own patterns of camouflage would halt immediately and that a more or less standard scheme would be applied to vehicles before they left the factories. The base colour of Dunkelgelb RAL 7028 would be retained, over which large patches of Olivgrün RAL 6003 and Rotbraun RAL 8017 were to be painted. Unlike the orders issued in the early years of the war, there was no detailed description of the extent or exact appearance of the camouflage patches and most seem to have been cloud-like in shape with high-contrasting, hard edges. Interestingly, the camouflage patterns seen on Panthers assembled at this time, although similar, commonly feature soft edges and this may be merely a preference of the manufacturer. The order stressed that every effort was to be made to deliver the remaining August consignment in the factory applied camouflage although the number of Tiger II tanks this affected can have been no more than ninety-four, the complete production figure for the month.

This period also saw the introduction of the so-called Ambush Scheme where dots of contrasting colour were painted onto the camouflage patches. Again, the dots could have a soft edge, as if painted with a spray gun, or hard edges, as though they were applied with a brush. Examples of these patterns are shown in the Camouflage and Markings section. Most sources suggest that the Ambush Scheme was short-lived but examples are seen among the last production batch which left the assembly lines in March 1945 and it seems that not all the tanks painted with the large patches of Olivgrün and Rotbraun were given the contrasting dots. It may have been that the dots were a refinement that was neglected when production targets needed to be met. At

Notes

1. As with most German camouflage colours this shade was rushed into service and did not receive an official RAL code for some time. The subsequent OKH order of 3 April 1943 advised that it would henceforth be known as Dunkelgelb RAL 7028. The RAL colour system and the colours used by the German army are discussed in detail in the tenth book in this series *Tiger I: German Army heavy tank, Southern Front North Africa, Sicily and Italy.* The RLM system was used by the Luftwaffe.

2. The Heereswaffenamt was the army's ordnance office. The Amtsgruppe für Industrielle Rüstung-Waffen und Gerat 6, or Wa J Rü-WuG 6, was the branch concerned with the manufacture of weapons systems, specifically tanks and tractors.

Examples of the variation possible with camouflage patterns applied by units in the field. At left: Painted with broad bands of Rotbraun and Olivgrün, very little of the Dunkelgelb base is visible on this Tiger II of schwere Panzer-Abteilung 503 photgraphed in October 1944. At right: The soft mottled pattern here is barely discernible. A number of sources mention that the paint was more easily worn off when the paste had been mixed with water.

Examples of what must have been some of the first and last tanks painted in a factory applied schemes. At left: Tigers of 1.Kompanie, schwere Panzer-Abteilung 503 photographed in late September 1944. At right: One of the last tanks to leave the Henschel factory in March 1945. This vehicle is discussed in detail on page 26.

the end of the first week of September 1944 the Heereswaffenamt ordered all manufacturers to immediately cease the application of Zimmerit, the anti-magnetic mine paste which had been introduced just over a year before, and although exact weekly production figures for Henschel are not available, a number of tanks would have been painted in the new camouflage pattern, perhaps the Ambush Scheme, after receiving a coat of Zimmerit.

On 31 October 1944 a directive issued by the Heeres-Abnahmestelle II(K) stipulated that Henschel was to cease the use of Dunkelgelb RAL 7028 as a base colour for armoured vehicles. Tanks were from now on to be painted in a camouflage scheme made up of patches of Braun, Grün and Gelb over the basic red oxide primer (1). Curiously the order went on to state that if Dunkelgelb was not available, Dunkelgrau RAL 7021 was a permissible alternative although these two colours are at almost opposite ends of the spectrum. Ideally, however, stocks of Dunkelgrau were to be conserved suggesting that its use in the future was at least being contemplated. It seems that this order may have been the formalisation of a practice that had begun at the Henschel plant in the previous September at around the time Zimmerit was discontinued. At least one Tiger II, Fgst. Nr. 280243 which was completed on 11 September 1944, was painted in Rot Oxide RAL 8012 over which irregular stripes of Olivgrün and Dunkelgelb were sprayed. On 29 November 1944 the Heereswaffenamt advised vehicle manufacturers that a new system was to be introduced where the armour components were to be painted in a base coat of Dunkelgrün RAL 6003 before they were delivered to the assembly plants. Once assembly was completed the tank would be camouflaged by the addition of Rotbraun RAL 8017 and Dunkelgelb RAL 7028 painted in sharp contours. In the case of the Tiger II this would mean of course that the final camouflage scheme would be applied at the Henschel plant before the tank was accepted by the Heereswaffenamt.

This scheme was not to come into effect until 1 March 1945, probably in anticipation of the approaching winter months.

However, on 20 December 1944 a new order directed that the painting of armour components in Dunkelgrün RAL 6003 was to begin immediately only to be followed by another directive dated 23 January 1945 advising manufacturers that existing paint stocks could be used until 30 May 1945, provided that theyw ere not thinned. It was anticipated that the new camouflage would be in general use by June 1945.

Heeres-Memorandum, Anstrich des Heeresgerät dated 25 December 1944 went into more detail and Heeres-Verordnungsblatt Nr.52 of 3 February 1945 brought all these orders together reiterating that base coat was to be Dunkelgrün RAL 6003, camouflaged with Rotbraun and Dunkelgelb applied in equal amounts (2). The camouflage was to be completed after final assembly and a template or guide was provided. Interestingly, the dark yellow colour is referred to as Dunkelgelb RAL 7028 Ausgabe 1944 suggesting that this shade may have been somehow different to the colour stipulated in April 1943 (3). The order went on to state that although the use of Dunkelgelb as a base colour was to stop immediately, deliveries to front line units were not to be delayed due to the lack of suitable colour paint. How many Tigers were painted according to this order is not known and if the new scheme did come into effect on 1 March 1945, as intended, the figure could not have been more than thirty tanks.

1. The Heeres-Abnahmestelle was a branch of the Heereswaffenamt responsible for the acceptance of equipment. The office mentioned here had responsibilty for the Hannover area. The names used for the colours here are transcribed exactly as they are recorded in the order, although the correct RAL numbers, 8017, 6003 and 7028 respectively, were used. Similarly RAL 7021 is referred to as Grau.

2. Heeres-Verordnungsblatt were orders dealing with unclassified information.

3. The exact shade of Dunkelgelb and the use of this colour has perhaps generated more debate than any other aspect of German tank development.

Dragon Models Ltd
B1-10/F., 603-609 Castle Peak Rd.
Kong Nam Industrial Building
Tsuen Wan, N. T., Hong Kong.
www.dragon-models.com

Dragon USA
1315 John Reed Ct, City of Industry,
CA 91745, USA
www.dragonmodelsusa.com

Tamiya Inc
Shizuoka City, Japan
www.tamiya.com

Trumpeter
NanLong Industrial Park,SanXiang,
ZhongShan,GuangDong, China
www.trumpeter-china.com

Hobby Boss
NanLong Industrial Park,SanXiang,
ZhongShan,GuangDong, China
www.hobbyboss.com

Academy Plastic Models
521-1, Yonghyeon-dong, Uijeongbu-si,
Gyeonggi-do, Korea
www.academy.co.kr

Hobby Fan/ AFV Club
6F ., No.183, Sec. 1, Datong Rd, Xizhi City
Taipei County 221, Taiwan
www.hobbyfan.com

Royal Model
Via E. Montale, 19-95030 Pedara, Italy
www.royalmodel.com

Italeri S.p.A.
via Pradazzo 6/b
40012 Calderara di Reno
Bologna, Italy
www.italeri.com

Rye Field Models
www.ryefield-model.com
An almost non-existent website. I would recommend one of the on-line retailers.

Hauler
Jan Sobotka
Moravská 38
620 00 Brno
Czech Republic
Www.hauler.cz

Voyager
Room 501, No.411 4th Village
SPC Jinshan District
Shanghai 200540
P.R.China
www.voyagermodel.com

Griffon Model
Suite 501, Bldg 01, 418 Middle Longpan
Road, Nanjing, China
www.griffonmodel.com
Since writing this book Griffon have added a number of Tiger items to their catalogue

Aber
ul. Jalowcowa 15, 40-750 Katowice, Poland
www.aber.net.pl

E.T. Model
www.etmodeller.com

Friulmodel
H 8142. Urhida, Nefelejcs u. 2., Hungary
www.friulmodel.hu

Modelkasten
Chiyoda-ku Kanda, Nishiki-Cho 1-7, Tokyo,
Japan
www.modelkasten.com
Very difficult to navigate but worthwhile.

Eduard Model Accessories
Mirova 170, 435 21 Obrnice
Czech Republic
www.eduard.com

Master Club
www.masterclub.ru
It appears that this firm is closely associated with Armour35 a Russsian mail-order company.

Model Artisan Mori
Yasutsugu Mori
Maison Suiryu 302, Kunoshiro-cho 1-10
Yokkaichi-City, Mie 510-0072, Japan
www.artisanmori.web.fc2.com

Model Factory Hiro
Yubinbango 121-0063 Adachi-ku, Tokyo
Higashihokima 2-Chome, 3-8 Japan
www.modelfactoryhiro.com

RB Model
Powstancow Wlkp.29B
64-360 Zbaszyn
Poland
www.rbmodel.com

M Workshop Singapore
91 Bencoolen St Sunshine Plaza01-58
Singapore
www.themworkshop.com

Zvezda (Zvezda-America)
www.zvezda-usa.com
Note that the Russian catalogue is not the same as the US version.

ROCHM Model
www.rochmmodel.com
Rochmmodel@gmail.com
This company has a huge selection of parts and accessories for 1/35 scale Tiger models including sets to build specific vehicles.

As with the previous book in this series I have endeavoured to give the reader an understanding of a complex subject and provide the modeller with the inspiration to create a scale representation of what is arguably the most famous armoured vehicle to take to the battlefield. In researching this project I consulted a number of works but no book on the Tiger tanks could be written without reference to the *Germany's Tiger Tanks* volumes by Hilary L. Doyle and the late Thomas L. Jentz. I also drew heavily on the works of Oberst Wolfgang Schneider, particularly his histories of the Tiger battalions, and to a lesser extent the books of Waldemar Trojca , Horst Scheibert, Jacek Solarz and Franz Kurowski. An invaluable resource are Thomas Jentz's *Panzertruppen* books which I would recommend to any reader with an interest in German armour of the Second World War period. I would also recommend *Tiger* by Egon Kleine and Volkmar Kühn although it is difficult to obtain and has only been published in German.I should also acknowledge Hartmut von Holdt of Tiger im Focus for his many insightful observations, and the contributors to the Axis History and the Feldgrau forums, especially Martin Block and the late Ron Klages whose research on unit histories and vehicle allocations would fill many volumes. I would like to thank Lester Plaskitt, Steve Shrimpton and Sheng Hui who very generously allowed me to publish the images of their work. I am indebted to Rupert Harding and Stephen Chumbley at Pen & Sword for their advice, assistance and above all patience. Of the product manufacturers I must make special mention of Roberto Reale of Royal Model, Sheng Hui of ROCHM, Jan Zdiarsky from Eduard Accessories and Freddie Leung of Dragon Models who all helped enormously. As always, I am indebted to Karl Berne, Valeri Polokov and J.Howard Parker for their invaluable assistance with the photographs and period insignia.